THE BIG BRASS RING

An Original Screenplay by
ORSON WELLES

with Oja Kodar

BLACK SPRING PRESS

First published in a limited edition of 1000 copies by Santa Teresa
Press, Santa Barbara, 1987.

This edition published by Black Spring Press, 1991

Black Spring Press Ltd.
63 Harlescott Road
London SE15 3DA

A catalogue record for this book is available
from the British Library.

Printed and bound in Great Britain by
The Guernsey Press Co. Ltd., Guernsey, Channel Islands.

ISBN 0 948238 16 X

PREFACE

There has been little public opportunity to study Orson Welles's gifts as a writer. Some Welles magazine articles, prefaces to books, and some short plays, can be found by the diligent. The novel, *Mr Arkadin*, which bears Welles's name (and long presumed to be the basis of his film) was disowned by him as it is actually an adaptation of Welles's screenplay by French writer, Maurice Bessy.

Welles's extensive talents as a screenwriter have been even further hidden. Of the numerous screenplays he is known to have written, almost nothing has been available to be read. The published screenplays for *The Trial* (Simon & Schuster, 1970) and *Touch of Evil* (Rutgers University Press, 1985) are actually reconstructed cutting continuities, rather than actual shooting scripts, and were created after the completion of the films. The only Welles shooting script published has been *Citizen Kane* (*The Citizen Kane Book*, Little Brown, 1971). Ironically, the presentation of the *Kane* script is marred by Pauline Kael's accompanying essay, "Raising Kane," a very sloppy attempt at film scholarship. Her essay which tries to promote the talents of Herman J. Mankiewicz boldly asserts that Welles did not write any portion of the *Kane* script. This serious charge was made without any attempt to do the necessary extensive research or interview Welles to obtain a fuller view. With his skillful study of the RKO Pictures Archives, Robert Carringer in his *The Making of Citizen*

Kane (University of California Press, 1985) not only shows the improperly formulated Kael position to be false but indicates in detail the great importance of Welles's contributions to the shooting script.

The Big Brass Ring, written over forty years later towards the end of Welles's career, provides not only an excellent study forum for Welles's abilities as a writer but is invigorating reading. Its classic Wellesian themes including politics, Spain, friendship, the perception of success and failure, combine with strong echoes of *Citizen Kane*. The film was conceived to be produced in black and white. Orson Welles intended to play the role of Kim Menaker, with Oja Kodar portraying the character Cela Brandini.

§

Jonathan Rosenbaum, in his afterword, will provide an extensive essay relating at length the complete history of the screenplay and its importance in the larger context of Welles's career as a filmmaker. He will show just how very close the film came to being made only to turn finally elusive. *The Big Brass Ring* should be initially encountered and hopefully enjoyed as the finished and self-contained work that it is. The strengths of the screenplay and its triumph as a piece of art need not be clouded on first impression by the machinations of the Hollywood process which restrained it from being recreated into another important work of art; an Orson Welles film.

§

The contributions to the creation of this book have been numerous. Oja Kodar graciously answered our many questions. Besides allowing the screenplay's publication, she is owed a great debt for her strong efforts to preserve the many facets of the Orson Welles legacy. Bill Krohn was of great aid in seeing the project reach print and shared his valuable insights. Henry Jaglom provided much information on the history of the attempts to see the screenplay produced. Arnon Milchan took time to give his view as a film producer. Richard Wilson related his useful knowledge of Welles. Others aided the effort including, in no special order: Gary Graver, Don Cannon, John Cannon, Wayne Warga, Steven Gilbar, Peter L. Stern, Deborah Sanford, George E. Diskant, Christine Tamblyn, Dave Kehr, Victor Fuentes, James Curtis, Brian Kirby, Thomas Elsaesser, James Gourley, Charles Wolfe, Steven A. Stilwell, Todd McCarthy, John Kurten, Howard Rodman, and Sasha Newborn.

JAMES PEPPER

THE BIG BRASS RING

FADE IN:

A montage — or maybe a filmed collage is more accurate

BLAKE PELLARIN FOR PRESIDENT . . .
Time and dust and weather have smudged and wilted the famous
Pellarin grin in the tatters of old campaign posters still to be glimpsed
in those few dead ends and forgotten corners of the country where
nobody bothers to sweep such stuff away.

Over this, roll:

        MAIN TITLE

       and principal credits

1

1. INTERIOR. NEW YORK LUXURY HOTEL – THE BAR – NIGHT
(STUDIO)

An appreciative, expensive-looking little crowd has been watching
President Reagan . . . He bobs his head, says, "Thank you,," and,
as the bartender turns off the television, there is a round of light
but warm applause.

An outstanding couple in this audience is SENATOR and MRS.
PELLARIN. Most eyes turn toward them now, and the tall, young-
looking Democrat is seen to be clapping his hands along with
everyone else . . . His handsome wife stands motionless, staring at
the empty TV tube.

The maitre d', easily catching their attention, waves the couple forward into:

2. INTERIOR. LARGE, GLAMOROUS DINING ROOM (CRANE
SHOT)

A certain cheerful alacrity in following him suggests the possibility
that they have paused to hear Mr. Reagan mainly because it wouldn't
have been very gracious not to . . .

And gracious is the world for them. Smiles of personal recognition
and general acknowledgement are distributed like roses as they process through the buzzing diners to their table . . .

Someone begins to clap . . . others join in, and suddenly the whole
room is on its feet applauding.

They stand for a moment: the Senator grinning his famous grin, his
lovely wife flushed with happiness and pride. Then they sit down,
and the restaurant returns to normalcy, except for a heightened murmur on every side.

A busboy (Mexican or Puerto Rican) bringing them ice water, looks
furtively around, then quickly whispers in Pellarin's ear.

                    DIANA
What did he say?

                    PELLARIN
He said he voted for me.

Her answer comes, almost ventriloquially, from between clenched
but smiling teeth:

DIANA

What goddamn primary was that. . . ?

QUICK FADE OUT.

3. INTERIOR. THE SITTING ROOM IN THE PELLARINS' SUITE OF
CABINS—DAY

GIGI ANDRADE, a merry widow in her late seventies, is the owner
of the grandest yacht afloat (unless you count the Greeks—and who
does anymore?). She and Diana are playing backgammon.

DIANA

. . . and after that, we even lost in Dayton.

GIGI

Yes, darling.

DIANA

Never mind—we'll carry it, next time around.

GIGI

Yes, darling.

Senator Blake Pellarin (now sprouting the beginnings of a beard)
is stretched out on a sofa, doing his damnedest not to listen to his
wife . . . Diana has been for many seasons, high on the list of the
Ten Best Dressed Women in the World. One of her bitchier friends
has said that she's the Texas answer to the Duchess of Windsor.

DIANA

A *brokered* convention, of course, which we had every
reason to expect—would have had to mean a shoo-in for
us on the third ballot . . .

GIGI

Yes, darling.

Pretending to read a book, Pellarin is bored to distraction. He's done
nothing on this yachting trip but grow a beard. The beard is a failure;
Ronnie's in the White House—and tomorrow (when they make port
in Tangiers) Blake has half a mind to jump ship.

As far back as he can remember, people have been telling Blake that
he was born to be the President of the United States. In school he
was the best in everything; the handsomest . . . He never seemed
to have a choice in the matter.

3

Born in Whipple Butte, Texas (where the Pellarins have been pretty much in charge of things since the days of Sam Houston) Blake is, however, trained by a Harvard education, but keeps his considerable intelligence discreetly muted on the hustings. There's plenty of real, down-home, country-cured Texas in our candidate, who, at a county fair, or any such appropriate occasion, can cornball it with the best.

Diana Pellarin, lusting mightily for the first ladyship of the land, and sustained by an ecstatic hatred of Nancy Reagan, stands firm in her conviction that fate has, with an indelible pencil, marked her man for the biggest job on the planet . . . the next time around.

She has been ever at the candidate's side, clinging to his every public word, and gazing up at him with those huge, tirelessly adoring eyes, which, to her husband, have long since resembled nothing so much as a pair of lightly poached eggs.

DIANA
(to Gigi)
Teddy's got that big Boston ass of his stuck in his Senate seat. He's already making noises — he just isn't making sense.

GIGI
Yes, darling.

The Senator puts down his book, rises, and with a stifled yawn, moves to a porthole and peers glumly out at nothing.

The backgammon continues . . .

If indeed, the burden of a great destiny is his, he carries it lightly, in his own easygoing style. But this presidential candidate is a two-time loser, and those who know him best aren't certain what this last defeat has done to him.

He wanders aimlessly into:

4. THE ADJOINING CABIN (THE BEDROOM)

When Pellarin sees what's happening here he freezes —

The Young Girl who, just recently, had been giving Mrs. Pellarin a pedicure, is, at this moment, bent over the dressing table. She has opened Diana's jewel case and is holding in her hands the necklace with the famous Pellarin emeralds. When she catches sight of Pellarin in the looking glass, she freezes, too.

They stare at each other in total silence.

4

Then Pellarin very carefully closes the door.

In the other cabin, the shrill, gossiping voices of the two women can still be heard, just partly muffled by the closed door. This birdhouse noise would seem to have sustained in him some secret but curiously pleasing decision.

He sits down after a long moment, his eyes still locked in those of the young thief . . . Blake is a notorious womanizer. But just here he's not interested in sex. It is the act itself — the theft — which fascinates him.

PELLARIN

Keep it.

She searches his face. Another tense moment . . . What she reads assures her that this crazy passenger really means it. He even pantomimes stuffing the necklace down the front of her uniform. Fumbling, she does just that.

A door leads from the stateroom to the outside passageway; he opens it and stands there, waiting for her to leave.

She sidles out, her eyes filled with a lingering, unintelligent suspicion.

The Senator is left alone. He gives himself a sidelong glance in the mirror . . .

Just who is it that he sees? — Blake Pellarin *looks* honest . . . Maybe a bit too handsome to be considered altogether trustworthy. But we all have our handicaps . . . Undoubtedly, he *sounds* honest. As a political performer his command of television can only be compared to Roosevelt's mastery of radio.

For now we'll leave our hero where he stands — slightly avoiding his own image in the mirror.

Senator Pellarin has, for the moment, joined the criminal class, and seems to be enjoying it.

DISSOLVE:

5.   SERIES OF SCENES (SILENT) ABOARD THE YACHT — NIGHT

Pellarin searching for the manicurist . . . from the engine room to the radio shack . . . Pellarin (rashly) giving a message to the Steward . . . Pellarin in earnest and amicable conversation with the Chef . . .

DISSOLVE:

6.   INTERIOR. THE CHEF'S CABIN—NIGHT

Unlike the steward, the ship's Chef de Cuisine has been richly bribed;
and himself a gay old dog at heart, is lending Pellarin his cabin. Here
the rendezvous has been arranged, and here Pellarin finds her waiting
for him . . .

A tense silence after they're alone.

Then Pellarin attempts an explanation . . . She strains to understand
(Portuguese is her only language, and Pellarin is addressing her in
a mixture of pidgin English and Border Spanish) . . . The tall, excited gentleman seems to be telling her—quite unnecessarily—that
she's in trouble . . .

                    PELLARIN
Don't you see. . . ? Eventually they're bound to get around
to searching you. We're in Tangiers tomorrow—don't go
ashore. Leave everything to me.

He starts away.

I'll find a fence for you, don't worry.

                    YOUNG GIRL
A . . . a fence? (Is this crazy gringo ready to give her his
wife's jewelry only to get laid?)

Her blank expression forces him to try a little clumsy pantomime
. . . no result.

                    PELLARIN
What's your name?

This she understands.

                    YOUNG GIRL
Tina.

Tina is a small brown girl from Recife and Blake's practiced eye can't
help but notice that she's really rather cute. Catching a glint of this,
and with astonishing speed, she starts to undress.

Untypically, he panics and dashes out before the striptease is
completed.

But not before he has snatched up the necklace!

CUT TO:

7. EXTERIOR. THE PORT OF TANGIERS — JUST BEFORE DAWN

There's no berth for the Andrade yacht, so it's dropping anchor off shore. Pellarin, carrying a small airplane bag, climbs down the rope ladder and lands neatly in the pilot's boat just as it pulls away.

A small dark face can be seen in one of the lower portholes — Tina, mournfully observing his departure.

DISSOLVE:

8. INTERIOR. THE AIRPORT IN TANGIERS (HALF AN HOUR LATER) — EARLY MORNING

Pellarin turns from the ticket counter and is confronted by an attractive and intense Italian lady.

> THE ITALIAN LADY
> (*making an announcement which*
> *seldom fails to impress*)
>
> I am Cela Brandini.

> PELLARIN
>
> Of course you are!

> CELA BRANDINI
>
> And I have never asked you for an interview —

> PELLARIN
>
> 'Guess I'm just plain lucky.

> CELA BRANDINI
>
> We'll have it when you're back. For now we just have time for coffee. I will buy it for you.

9. TRAVELING SHOT

She strides away in perfect confidence that she'll be followed — and she's right. Smiling a little to himself, Pellarin joins her at the coffee bar where she orders for them both — in Arabic.

> CELA BRANDINI
>
> There's no choice when you get to Chad: you'll have to take that little Cessna everybody charters. Then, if they let you through the border, there's just one hope: the Field Marshal will have a Jeep laid on to take you to the Capital. Have you got a gun?

7

PELLARIN
(*grinning*)
You're serious?

CELA BRANDINI
I'm always serious. It's dangerous country.

PELLARIN
I'm a U.S. Senator, Miss Brandini. We don't carry side arms.

CELA BRANDINI
Here's your coffee. Follow me.

He is amused again to find himself obediently at heel. They settle at the table of her choice.

PELLARIN
The way I hear it, you're the brightest lady in your business.

CELA BRANDINI
You hear correctly.

She unstraps an enormous bag from her shoulder, bringing out of it a pack of Gaulois cigarettes, a gold lighter and the very latest thing in tiny tape recorders.

PELLARIN
So why bother with *me*? I didn't even carry the Southwest. Just look at Connolly—

CELA BRANDINI
I don't give a damn for Connolly. He spent eleven million dollars and got himself one delegate. You may be more expensive, Pellarin, but we think that you were probably the best of all the bargains.

PELLARIN
And who is "we"?

CELA BRANDINI
A lot of people I've been talking to. You were way ahead in other places. If it weren't for Kennedy, I think you would have made it. Next time you really might . . . But of course, there's still the old business about Menaker—

8

A sudden and extreme drop of temperature . . .

She waits for a response . . .

The pause grows heavy as she realizes that none will be forthcoming . . .

DISSOLVE:

10. INTERIOR. THE YACHT — EARLY MORNING

GARNER STRICKLAND ("GARNE" as he is known to all his friends) is knocking discreetly on the door of Diana Pellarin's cabin.

> STRICKLAND
>
> Dinah . . .

(Diana's intimates — and even Blake — often call her "Dinah." Nobody seems to know why. Maybe it used to be her name.)

> STRICKLAND
>
> Are you up, darling?

> DIANA'S VOICE
>
> Yes. . . ?

> STRICKLAND
>
> Are you decent?

> DIANA'S VOICE
>
> The door's open.

11. INTERIOR. THE CABIN

Strickland finds her at her dressing table, completing her morning makeup. Her blouse is still laid out on one of the twin beds. Neither are embarrassed by the condition of her dress. His wife and Strickland are obviously intimates and, just as obviously, not lovers.

Garner Strickland has been a guest aboard the yacht since the beginning of the cruise. Well-born, well-connected and expensively educated, he had been intended for the diplomatic service. After some years *en poste* in various dreary corners of the globe, he gave it up for politics and was a failure. After that he attached himself to Mrs. Pellarin (whom he adores) as aide de campe and constant male companion. Too undersexed to join the Gay Liberation, he fulfills himself with the busy duties of this rather special relationship.

9

Diana rises. Strickland automatically picks up the (almost) see-through blouse and helps her on with it.

> STRICKLAND
> I wouldn't wear a jacket, love, it's sweltering already—

> DIANA
> You can carry it for me.

He does so; following her out—

CUT TO:

12. THE MAIN DECK OF THE YACHT—EARLY MORNING

Old Gigi is already up. Greetings are exchanged.

> STRICKLAND
> *(sotto voce)*
> No word about the emeralds?

> DIANA
> *(moving to the rail)*
> Who gives a shit about the emeralds?

> GIGI
> *(to Strickland)*
> She's so brave about it . . .
> *(turning to Diana)*
> Blake told somebody he thought he might have just *glimpsed* the robber sneaking out into the corridor . . . Wasn't in uniform, thank God. That gets my crew off the hook, anyway.

> STRICKLAND
> *(with a hard smile)*
> Well, Gigi, dear, that does narrow it straight down, doesn't it—to your guests?

> DIANA
> *(her back to them, at the rail)*
> Five . . . Blake's left us.

> STRICKLAND
> *(horrified)*
> Oh, my *God!*

GIGI
Before dawn, darling. He didn't even leave a note.

The STEWARD, who has been lurking discreetly in the background now comes forward, envelope in hand.

STEWARD
Excuse me, but he did leave this—

GIGI
*(snatching the note from him
and reading it aloud)*
"I know what you want from me, and you're going to get it! That's a promise."
(looking up, indignantly)
This isn't addressed to *me*—!

STEWARD
I thought you'd want to see it first, Madam.

STRICKLAND
(looking over her shoulder)
It says "Dear Tina—"

GIGI
(to Diana)
Tina?—you know Tina, darling—she gave you that nice pedicure . . .

STRICKLAND
(with a thin smile)
It seems that's not her only specialty—

He breaks off, sharply aware he's gone too far—especially in the presence of the Steward. He turns toward Diana. The others following his look . . .

Her hands on the railing, she stands there staring out at the chalk-white city through mirrored glasses. She hasn't moved.

DIANA
Garne—

STRICKLAND

Yes, dear?

He moves quickly to her side . . . Waits in vain for her to speak.
Then turns to give the others a meaning look. They understand, and
chatter away as gracefully as they can manage.

GIGI
(a vague murmur)
See you at lunch, darling . . .

STRICKLAND
(after they've all gone)
Gigi's right, you know — You're brave as hell.

DIANA
I'm frightened, Garne.
(thrusting a piece of
paper into his hand)
I'm frightened to death . . .

STRICKLAND
(bewildered)
What's this?

DIANA
All our people. Cable 'em. Get 'em on the phone. We need
everybody we can trust —

STRICKLAND
Here — ? Aren't we supposed to leave for Barcelona — ?
(he breaks off)
We ought to get in touch with the insurance people first — ?

DIANA
Blake went sneaking off this morning — Just stop and think
and tell me why.

STRICKLAND
Some nonsense with that little manicurist, I should think.
There'll be no scandal. They can't have gossip writers in a
Godforsaken hole like this.

12

DIANA

Not the girl — He didn't go off with her. I tell you this is
Africa — !

STRICKLAND
(after a slightly stunned silence)
It's not the Congo, darling. It's just a little Moorish port.
You make it sound like Blake is off into the Heart of
Darkness —

DIANA

That's it! That's just exactly where he's bound for . . .
(pause)
Garne! Pull yourself together.

This is precisely what he was about to say to her . . . (Has she been
drinking — this early in the day. . . ?)

DIANA (continued)
Use your brains for once! Who's been in Central Africa all
this year — ?
*(he opens his mouth, but she
cuts him off with the answer)*
The one man in the world that the Senator must never, *ever*
see again. . . .

Aghast, Strickland stares at her . . .

CUT TO:

13. INTERIOR. THE AIRPORT IN TANGIERS — MORNING

The loudspeaker is announcing (in Arabic and French) the imminent
departure of Pellarin's plane . . . He and Cela Brandini are still at
their table, with several empty coffee cups to witness how long they
have been talking. It's also evident that they've been getting along
well together . . . When he hears the announcement, Pellarin gets
to his feet. She rises, too, and their eyes meet.

CELA BRANDINI
*(they have been laughing at some
joke. Now she turns, serious)*
There's something you might as well know.

PELLARIN
(*still smiling*)
Must be bad news: you've saved it to the last minute—

CELA BRANDINI
I've just come from where you're going . . . I've just come
from Menaker.

Pause.

PELLARIN
How is he?

CELA BRANDINI
We did a lot of talking—

PELLARIN
I'll bet he did the most of it.

14. CRANE SHOT

They make their way through the crowd of Arabs, Berbers, and
tourists to the departure gate.

CELA BRANDINI
(*as they go*)
It would be hard to find a more impressive failure—

PELLARIN
Hold it—!

She stops. He goes on, sharply:

PELLARIN (continued)
This is *Doctor Kimball Menaker* we're speaking of—

The highly colored mass of travelers is boiling all around them . . .
He glares at her. She smiles at him . . . He can't help it, he smiles
back.

PELLARIN
Look, sugar—skin me alive just like you always do with
everybody—

CELA BRANDINI
Well, not *everybody*—

14

PELLARIN

But please—don't write that Kimball Menaker's a failure—

CELA BRANDINI

I write what I see . . .

PELLARIN

He really should have made it—into the history books, I
mean. He could have been our Churchill.

CELA BRANDINI

Let's sit down; these things never leave on time—

Together they nudge a path through the mob.

I almost liked the man—

PELLARIN

Almost?

CELA BRANDINI

Alright, I did. He's certainly unique . . .

They find an empty section of bench just by the gate. During this
her hand has gone to the tape recorder.

CELA BRANDINI (continued)

I'm trying to make sense of your relationship—

PELLARIN
(*ruefully*)

And I've been spending years trying to explain it.

CELA BRANDINI

To other journalists?

PELLARIN

To every tanktown nobody . . . to local TV interviewers—
talk show hosts—

CELA BRANDINI

A waste of time: they're cunts. All of them.

PELLARIN

It *is* pretty damn fatiguing, I'll admit—

15

CELA BRANDINI
We'd better get in line —

This last in response to a final announcement from the loudspeaker.

PELLARIN
You're not coming with me?

Indeed, in her canvas hat (G.I. issue) and her safari jacket, Cela looks much more like someone bound for the heart of Central Africa than he does.

CELA BRANDINI
No, I'll see you when you're back — if you come back.

He looks to see if she's kidding. It's hard to tell.

CELA BRANDINI (continued)
Tell me what's fatiguing.

PELLARIN
Fighting for the chance to talk a little sense. Scratching for an inch of news space, for a few seconds of TV — trying to smuggle in some matter of policy or public interest. And each time getting blasted in the face with the same fucking question — If you'll pardon the use of the word "question."

She looks at him through narrowed, green, intelligent eyes. She suddenly knows that she likes him — very much. And that it's mutual.

CELA BRANDINI
It's been quite a while now since you've seen that man —

PELLARIN
Much too long.

She raises the little tape recorder, holding it near his ear and turning on the playback.

CELA BRANDINI
Or — heard his voice.

What issues from the small machine is loud and clear. It quickly captures an attentive audience of waiting passengers. Cela watches Pellarin's delighted reaction . . .

16

MENAKER'S VOICE (on the tape recorder)
. . . A message? Do I wish to send a message to the Senator
from Texas? ex-chairman of the Foreign Affairs Commit-
tee? former vedette of the Hasty Pudding Club Review, our
future President, and my former friend?

A slight pause. Pellarin waits . . . Then the recorded voice of
Menaker, in a rumbling bass-baritone, is heard half-singing, half-
reciting the following inconsequential doggerel:

"The days of chivalry are dead,
Of which in stories I have read,
When knights were bold and acted kind of scrappy,
They used to take a lot of pains,
And fight all day to please their Janes,
And if their dame was tickled they was happy . . .

Pellarin is convulsed. She cuts off the machine.

CELA BRANDINI
Just what was *that* about?

PELLARIN
A very corny private joke.

CELA BRANDINI
And this "Hasty Pudding"?

PELLARIN
Students in our university. We do a kind of musical review
and, back in nineteen twenty-nine, that number you've just
heard was sung by young Kim Menaker—in sequins, a
blonde wig, a wimple and a lovely silver gown. He did three
encores. He still keeps doing 'em. And I don't know why,
it always slays me.

She is not amused.

CELA BRANDINI
I'm not writing about Dr. Menaker.

PELLARIN
I wish you were.

17

CELA BRANDINI

That interview was just for background.
                    (*she gives him the recorder*)
If you want to, take it with you on your trip . . . To keep
you company.

PELLARIN

Where do I return it?

CELA BRANDINI
                    (*looking at him thoughtfully*)
I *might* arrange a helicopter . . .

PELLARIN

Just to pick up that little bitty tape recorder? Golly gee,
Missy, you do live it up!

CELA BRANDINI

We've got to save your friend. That's why you're going, isn't
it? This goddamn Field Marshal's a bloody lunatic: he chops
off heads.

Pellarin stands up.

The part I *wanted* you to hear was what he said about the
Spanish War . . . The friend of Menaker was in the brigade
my father fought in.
                    (*she rises*)
And *apropos* of fathers, the way he speaks of you — he seems
to think he's *yours*.

Pellarin considers this with evident pleasure.

She studies him for a moment. What could have been mere rhetoric
has surprised her by its simplicity and truth.

CELA BRANDINI

And yet, politically — he almost killed you off.

PELLARIN

He didn't quite do that, you know . . . He killed himself.

Slight pause.

Another urgent announcement on the loudspeaker, at which he
dashes off — And just in time . . .

18

She watches this with interest . . .

DISSOLVE:

15. EXTERIOR. THE POSTAL AND TELEGRAPHIC BUILDING IN
TANGIERS — DAY

Jerry Kinzel is waiting impatiently in front of the main entrance . . .
Diana enters scene, with Garner Strickland in attendance.

> KINZEL
> (*a bit breathless*)
> Hi, everybody. I caught that early ferry from Algeciras. If
> Susie and I hadn't just *happened* to be on a little holiday —

> DIANA
> (*briskly cutting him off*)
> Susie?

> KINZEL
> My wife.

> DIANA
> (*with severity*)
> She isn't with you?

> KINZEL
> Christ, no; I left her in Marbella. She's perfectly happy —

> DIANA
> Her happiness is not what we're here to discuss —

> KINZEL
> (*quickly*)
> The first minute I got your message I came running —

> DIANA
> (*interrupting again, as she
> turns to Strickland*)
> And Mister Benart?

> STRICKLAND
> There we're lucky, too, darling. As it happens, Dinty is in
> Europe, too —

                            DIANA
Where?

                          STRICKLAND
The trouble is there's no night flight from London to
Tangiers . . .

                            DIANA
                  (*handing him a thick sheaf of forms*)
Send these cables to the others.

                          STRICKLAND
You don't want *all* these people, darling: they're in
America—

                            DIANA
Send them anyway.

Strickland hurries into the post office.

                            KINZEL
                  (*still dizzy with travel, but*
                  forcing a certain air of verve)
Just leave it to us, Mrs. Pellarin. Garne and I—we can take
care of anything that seems to be the trouble . . .

Diana looks at him.

                            KINZEL
I just wondered how I could be useful . . .

His voice fades, and falls silent under the weight of her hauteur.

                        KINZEL (continued)
I have my contacts, as you know . . .

Once ingloriously on the payroll of the CIA, Jerry encourages the
impression that he's still an intimate advisor to "The Company."
Strickland, who goes back to the more patrician OSS, knows better. In fact, Kinzel's private firm provides industrial espionage, and
Jerry also dabbles in some rather dubious operations on the international scene (privately funded), and likes to think of this as part
of "The Great Game."

They turn at the sound of a strong, lightly accented woman's voice:

                              20

THE VOICE

Your husband . . .

DIANA

Yes? What about him?

CELA BRANDINI

He left this morning, in great secrecy, for the Interior —

DIANA

Oh, yes, we *know* — But what a peculiar way of putting it.
The Senator is speaking at that Third World Conference on
nutrition —

CELA BRANDINI
(cutting in)

Last Monday it was finished.

DIANA
(sweetly)

I think you may have got that wrong —

CELA BRANDINI

No. I was there.

DIANA
(looking keenly at her opponent)

Your face — it *is* somehow familiar . . .

CELA BRANDINI

My name is.

KINZEL
*(pleased to find a role for himself
in this little scene)*

You're the Brandini woman!

CELA BRANDINI
(parodying Diana)

What a peculiar way of putting it.

KINZEL
(recovering something of his professional menace)

Quite a coincidence — bumping into you, like this —

DIANA
(taking charge again)
My Senator? How nice. We did so much enjoy that thing
you did on *Teddy* —
(a bit archly, but with no effort to charm)
But I can't hope that we'll be all that fond of what you'll
do to *us*.

CELA BRANDINI
(after a brief, chilly silence)
I'd like to see you *with* your husband.

DIANA
Then you *must* dine with us the moment he comes back —

CELA BRANDINI
You sail tonight.

DIANA
Ah, yes — we do.

CELA BRANDINI
Your next port's Barcelona.

DIANA
So it is.
(another icy little pause)
I expect that he'll be joining us in Barcelona.

CELA BRANDINI
(cutting in)
Mrs. Pellarin — I think you know just where he's bound for
now — *And* who it was he went to visit —

She stops as Garner Strickland comes out of the post office. They
exchange unfriendly looks. She turns and goes.

DIANA
(with muted rage)
Find out about that woman —

STRICKLAND
(at her side)
Brandini? A complicated dago bitch.

22

KINZEL

We got a file on her at Langley ten feet long . . .

Strickland sniffs a bit at this, but holds his peace.

KINZEL (continued)
(*darkly*)
We sure know who she *is* —

STRICKLAND

Yes, and so does everybody who can read — in any language, including Japanese.

KINZEL

I want to know just what she's up to. No damn good at all.

Slight pause.

DIANA

And the Senator?

KINZEL

What about him?

DIANA

He's disappeared.

KINZEL

You're kidding — !

He breaks off in the sudden, full realization that Diana Pellarin is never going to "kid" with Jerry Kinzel.

DIANA
(*turning to Strickland*)
No doubt about it — he's gone to see that awful man.

KINZEL

Which awful man?

STRICKLAND
(*in lowered tones*)
The awful man.

After a brief silence.

23

Not. . . ?

A hard-eyed look from Diana confirms it . . . all present are aghast.

DISSOLVE:

16. SERIES OF SHOTS: (AFRICA) BLAKE PELLARIN'S LONG TRIP—DAY

On different planes, he diverts himself by listening to the little tape machine . . . Over the shifting scenes of Africa he hears:

MENAKER'S VOICE: . . . As a science, economics is on the level with phrenology—the hope is for a tiny boom. But then we'll all be waiting for the giant bust.

BRANDINI'S VOICE: Then enter Pellarin on a white horse?

MENAKER'S VOICE: God knows who'll be on that horse, Brandini—but he'll be somebody Blake Pellarin will have to run against . . . Plus a coalition of bible thumpers and survivalists.

BRANDINI'S VOICE: Survivalists? . . .

MENAKER'S VOICE: Surely you've heard of *them*: the stockpilers of machine guns and canned food, all ready to repel the hungries and the commie hordes. They're digging hidey-holes up in the high hills and practicing how to fight off the Apocalypse . . . There'll be a lot of those, and none of 'em vote for Blake. Not if the cities start to burn.

BRANDINI'S VOICE: Then what hope is there for him?

MENAKER'S VOICE: The world is full of fools and liars. Quite often they're the ones in charge. Like the rest of us, when that happens, all that a president can do is buy a ticket for the show.

BRANDINI'S VOICE: And the alternative?

MENAKER'S VOICE: The President takes charge.

BRANDINI'S VOICE: On his white horse.

MENAKER'S VOICE: (*laughter.*)

DISSOLVE:

17. INTERIOR. A MOORISH COFFEE HOUSE – NIGHT

(The usual local color – maybe more so) . . . Diana Pellarin's little staff of snoopers hasn't been getting very far with its investigations . . . For reasons of security they're gathered here, drinking warm bottles of Coca-Cola . . .

Fat little DINTY BENART, the popular press secretary, is the latest to arrive, and the first with anything resembling hard information.

> DINTY
> I found the travel agent – the Senator's booked through to just about as close as he can get . . .
> > (*he pauses to catch his breath*)

> STRICKLAND
> Get to *what*, Dinty?

> DINTY
> Kurobe.

> STRICKLAND
> Where's Kurobe, for God's sake?

> DINTY
> Garner – it's the capital of the goddamn country.

> KINZEL
> > (*wisely*)
> They must have changed the name.

> STRICKLAND
> From what?

> KINZEL
> From . . . whatever it was, naturally. I'll have to check. We must have assets in there from before the coup.

> STRICKLAND
> And what's your famous "asset" going to do for *us*? Go tell the Senator his wife would like him to come home?

25

KINZEL

Shit, Garner—this is serious.

STRICKLAND

I'm *being* serious. There could be photographs—

DINTY

Jesus, yes—And what about TV!

KINZEL

That asshole of a country's the hell and gone from anywhere
. . . If we *could* get the Senator *delayed*, somehow . . . or
detoured for a day or so, I could send somebody in ahead
of him who'd get to Menaker—

STRICKLAND

And do what—? "terminate" the old fart, as you people say,
"without prejudice"?

KINZEL
(*after a moment, solemnly*)
You never heard me say it.

QUICK DISSOLVE TO:

18. INTERIOR. LIGHT PLANE—DAY

Blake Pellarin is on the last lap of his journey by air . . . and as his
light chartered plane is getting ready to land, he is, again, listening
to the voice of his friend.

MENAKER'S VOICE: (ON THE TAPE) . . . Franklin
Roosevelt ran half the world and then some with a personal
staff of nine people. Now they have five hundred.

BRANDINI'S VOICE: And you were one of nine—a
presidential advisor?

MENAKER'S VOICE: Oh, Mr. Roosevelt sometimes let you
think that's what you were. He had the great politico's art
of *listening* . . . Lyndon was the *talker*—nonstop. But
Johnson did collect his own small circle of intelligent
listeners, almost exclusively from Texas. That's where my
own star pupil got to shine . . .

26

BRANDINI'S VOICE: Blake Pellarin — the once and future candidate . . . So what happens next time around?

The plane bumps down on the tiny airfield. Pellarin turns off the tape recorder.

19.   THE PILOT
The border's over there. I'm stopping long enough for you to jump. If nobody's gonna keep you covered, you'd better start to run.

As Pellarin does —

QUICK DISSOLVE:

20. INTERIOR. LUXURY HOTEL — DAY

The penthouse suite of the Batunga Hilton gives little hint of conditions in the surrounding countryside. For an emerging state (even one so disastrously under-developed as this) a Hilton Hotel is the premier proof of status as a nation.

Two very tall and beautiful BLACK LADIES are playing, rather listlessly, a game of backgammon. Both mother-naked, and dressed only in their turbans. The infamous DR. KIMBALL MENAKER is in bed with a monkey.

Pellarin stands looking at him for a while in a silence disturbed only by the buzzing of flies, and the occasional muted whimper of the monkey.

                          MENAKER
She isn't well.

                          PELLARIN
Are you?

                          MENAKER
A wee bit thinner — I should hope.

                          PELLARIN
You smell of piss.

                          MENAKER
I claim no credit for that.
          (then, after a pause)
Why did you come here, Pellarin?

27

PELLARIN

You want the truth?

MENAKER

I can bear almost anything.

PELLARIN

Well . . . for one thing, I thought I'm here to make you
laugh.

MENAKER

That would be nice.
(*another pause*)
They got your wristwatch, didn't they?

PELLARIN

At the first checkpoint. Almost immediately.

MENAKER

Yes, they're awfully fond of wristwatches.

Pellarin's eyes move toward the backgammon players.

MENAKER (continued)
(*with a sort of ersatz leer*)
Handsome, aren't they. They're my bodyguards.

This is spoken with a certain, twisted pride.

PELLARIN

Could I ask you, as a favor, to please get out of bed.

MENAKER

Alas, I'm not at liberty to do so. Not just at the moment.
The explanation, I'm afraid, is rather delicate.

PELLARIN

About these women —

MENAKER

What about them?

PELLARIN

Are you at liberty to get them the hell out of here?

The old professor barks out a phrase or two in Swahili . . . The ladies, in perfect silence, and with the most unhurried and elegant gestures, help each other into their long, flowing robes: a kind of strip tease in reverse.

MENAKER

They'll have to wait outside the door.

PELLARIN

For what?

MENAKER

Not for you, young Pellarin. You would be ill-advised to interfere with those two creatures. They're far too interested in each other for any casual male canoodling; and they are truly dangerous. That's why the Field Marshal has set them to watch over me. He is, I needn't tell you, barking mad, and thinks of me as an enhancement to his world prestige, poor fellow.

PELLARIN

You're letting that monkey pee all over you.

MENAKER
(with bitter cheerfulness)
It's been going on for two days and a night. This last one, I must say, was rather long . . .

But I've had longer nights before.

Pellarin is uncomfortably aware of how true that last must be. He looks down sadly at the rumpled old gentleman in his filthy bed. By now the two women have left. The monkey seems to be asleep. It is very quiet in the room.

PELLARIN

Kim . . .

MENAKER

Yes, Boysie?

PELLARIN

You still think I failed you? Is that it? You think I ran away?

Menaker meets this with a smile.

29

MENAKER
I couldn't see you for the dust.

PELLARIN
I was running, all right—

MENAKER
We were just starting the campaign. Don't worry, Senator, you'll catch the big brass ring—next time around.

Silence.

PELLARIN
I've sort of missed you, you old fart . . .

MENAKER
It's good of you to say so. Pray understand that you're received here as a friend.

PELLARIN
That's how I came.

MENAKER
Yes, and at considerable danger to your person. This country (if we may call it that) is in a state of the most perfect anarchy. Did they get your wallet, too?

PELLARIN
Only the money—at something known as "currency control." So I guess I'm lucky.

MENAKER
Dear boy, you're lucky to be here alive.

PELLARIN
I'll say. Just look at what they missed—

Pellarin unbuttons his shirt.

MENAKER
Merciful God!

The open shirt reveals the glittering necklace draped around the Senator's neck.

MENAKER

I know those emeralds.

PELLARIN

Who doesn't? Certainly, nobody in Washington . . . Before
I tell you any more of this, I think I should explain that I'm
undoubtedly insane.

MENAKER

That's nice.

PELLARIN

At least it would be nice to hear you laugh . . .

Slight pause. Then —

DISSOLVE:

21.   EXTERIOR. THE DECK OF YACHT (AT SEA) — DAY

By now Diana's cohorts: a small combo of "image-makers," old campaign sidekicks, and a former member of the CIA — such as are immediately available — have come flying to her side. While they were
still in Tangiers, she had placed them under strict orders — to find
the Senator. After much feckless scuttling about, they have been
forced to admit to failure . . . What's worse, they have the unplea-
sant duty of reporting this to Mrs. Pellarin.

STRICKLAND

We do know where Menaker is, don't we?

KINZEL
(*darkly*)

And we know that he's in trouble.

Dinty Benart, that faithful old campaigner, steaming with sweat,
plunges on with his report.

DINTY

We hear there's still some shooting at the border. The airfield
in Kurobe's closed.

STRICKLAND

Oh, God, I thought *that* war was over.

31

KINZEL
(*looking, as usual, as though he knew a great deal
more than he's allowed to speak*)
It's what they want to have us *think* . . . I'll have to check
on that.

(Actually, intelligence on this situation has come to Kinzel strictly
from yesterday's newspaper.)

STRICKLAND
(*after a tense little silence*)
Blake certainly can't have forgotten that he's got that conference at the Hague. The Nobel's on his mind as much as
ours . . . Or ought to be.

DINTY
Then there's Brussels — Tuesday.

DIANA
There'll be the King. How can he miss *that*?

STRICKLAND
(*to Diana*)
He won't, darling.

KINZEL
(*gloomily*)
Don't be too sure. Our Great Man's in a kinda funny mood
these days. It wouldn't surprise me if he joined a monastery,
or started keeping bees.

Their faces flushed, the conspirators stare wide-eyed at each other.

DISSOLVE:

22. THE PENTHOUSE TERRACE ATOP THE BATUNGA
HILTON — SUNSET

The two old friends have moved out here from the penthouse
bedroom to catch a little of the evening breeze.

Blake Pellarin, finishing his story, is surprised to find a wide grin
on Kim Menaker's face.

PELLARIN
What are you so pleased about?

32

MENAKER

You. I'm happy to observe that after all these years of po-faced public service, the Senior Senator from the Great State of Texas is still capable of making a complete horse's ass of himself. I'm reassured. We may still have a President who's not *entirely* composed of plastic.

PELLARIN

That means you're going to help me?

MENAKER

Old darling, I had rather imagined you were here to help *me* . . . What are you looking for?

PELLARIN

I've got to find a fence. Obviously, I don't know where to look . . .

The wretched, ailing monkey still has his long thin arms clasped firmly around Menaker's neck.

MENAKER

"A fence." Meaning a receiver of stolen property?

PELLARIN

You know all that much better than I do, Kim. Aren't you an authority?

MENAKER

(*stating a simple fact*)

I'm an authority on everything.

PELLARIN

(*a bit impatient*)

On *crime*, dammit! I read that article of yours last year — all three parts of it: "The Criminal Underworld Considered as a Primitive Culture — An Anthropological View." . . . I've got that right, haven't I?

MENAKER

You've got it wrong. That was just a sketch for what I thought might someday be a chapter in another book I'm planning. Not enough field work, though: the data was too

33

thin — For one simple-minded moment I imagined you had
made this complicated and uncomfortable journey — at the
very least — to patch up an old friendship.

PELLARIN

Kim —

MENAKER
(*rumbling on*)
Instead, you've struggled all this way only to extract some
expert information from the King of Crooks.
(*he breaks off, his face darkening*)
Are you quite serious?

PELLARIN
Serious? I'm in one helluva spot —

Silence. Menaker is plunged in sudden gloom.

MENAKER
So am I, old darling.

Pellarin's face changes . . . The old man studies him . . .

MENAKER
You want to sell the necklace: go to Rome, to Bulgari's — or
Cartier's in Paris. They'll find one of those oil-soaked Arabs
for you, and get a price no fence could even think of.

PELLARIN
You think Diana wouldn't hear about it?

MENAKER
She hears everything. She has the celebrated Pellarin Mafia.
Officially, your staff, they all report to her.

PELLARIN
Not *all* of them.

MENAKER
Don't be too sure. She'll have her finger on your little thief
by now, we can be sure of *that*.

PELLARIN
Her name is Tina.

34

MENAKER

Let's call her Dulcinea. You've always had your Dulcineas.
A Quixote stricken with a raging case of satyriasis.

PELLARIN

I don't even *know* her, Kim. But I did make a promise . . .

MENAKER

You don't even know that she's a thief.

PELLARIN

I've made her one, haven't I? I'm her accomplice.

Menaker looks at him with a kind of awe. The sheer caprice of it
is positively dazzling. Here stands a man bent upon seeing to it that
a thief gets a fair price for what somebody might have stolen from
his own wife.

MENAKER

The girl means nothing to you?

PELLARIN

Less than nothing.

MENAKER

So it's the *promise* you're in love with? Why? Because you're
God's own little Eagle Scout.

PELLARIN

I don't know why, but in a way, I think the craziest promise is the sacred one.

Menaker looks at him with a certain air of respect.

MENAKER

Up in heaven, that's a line would probably receive a hearty
round of applause.

PELLARIN
(*with a grin*)

I'm kinda fond of it myself.

A brief silence.

MENAKER
(*making a decision*)
Boysie—it's just barely possible I'll meet up with you in
Spain.

PELLARIN
Spain?

MENAKER
There's a chance I can get out of here. But anyway, we'd
have to travel separately. And if you're going to smuggle
jewelry across a dozen international frontiers, you'll do that
little caper on your own.

PELLARIN
Why Spain?

MENAKER
You want to fence your pilfered loot—that's where we're
doing it.

Pellarin makes a vague gesture toward the clasp of the necklace.
Menaker stops him.

MENAKER
No, you get to wear the emeralds. They're most becoming.
And also . . .

Menaker detaches the little animal from his own chest and drapes
her delicately around Blake's neck, over the necklace.

MENAKER (continued)
You couldn't ask for better camouflage.

PELLARIN
A sick monkey?

MENAKER
Affectionate . . . misses her mother, so she'll never leave
your arms.

PELLARIN
She'll pee all over *me*.

36

MENAKER

Yes, that's something you can count on. She *is* quite sick,
poor little thing. She's sleeping now, but soon she'll be
rendering you quite unapproachable.

A pause . . . Dr. Menaker looks solemn. Then, with no change of
expression, he bursts into song:

MENAKER

"Nowadays the men are mild and meek;
They seem to have a yellow streak;
They never lay for other guys to flatten 'em;

Pellarin (not at all sure that the furry creature clinging to him has
not already commenced its promised function) gamely joins in:

PELLARIN AND MENAKER

"They think they've done a darned fine thing
If they just buy the girl a ring

(Pellarin, lacking the Professor's brio, is much nearer the pitch):

PELLARIN AND MENAKER

"Of imitation diamonds and platinum!"

The beautiful black bodyguards have come to the door. Whether
they are hoping for a party, or merely on the lookout for subver-
sion, it is hard to say.

The song over; and the two old friends look pleased with each other.

MENAKER

Be warned, young Pellarin — this whole thing could be a
scam.

PELLARIN

And I'm the sucker?

MENAKER

In the light of this current obsession with your given word,
I'd say that you're a set-up.

Pellarin grins at him.

PELLARIN
(*quoting from the song*)
"But then, the age of chivalry's not dead."

37

Menaker, an impressive figure in his filthy pajamas, has turned sud
denly grave.

MENAKER

Apart from all the *schweinerei* about the jewels, I'd like to
know how much you've changed. Or haven't changed . . .
I'm serious: What's left in you?

PELLARIN

What do you think?

MENAKER

Can you still love?

A long silence.

PELLARIN

I still do . . . You met her once yourself.

MENAKER

In Paris?

PELLARIN

That's where it was.

For some obscure reason, Menaker is absolutely delighted.

MENAKER

Then of course — we're going to Madrid!

QUICK FADE OUT.

QUICK FADE IN:

23.   A NIGHT SCENE with a dark glitter of water, the whole obscured
      by rain. (Perhaps the vague silhouette of the Columbus statue.) . . .

      Over this superimpose the title:

BARCELONA

24.   EXTERIOR. THE FAR END OF THE BARCELONA YACHT
      CLUB — NIGHT

      Black and windy . . . the figure of a woman can be made out stand-
      ing in the lee of a big packing case. She's struggling to light a cigarette,
      but stops as she sees Pellarin.

He's trudging along toward the dock, travel-worn and not in a good temper. The monkey, shivering in the cold, is clinging to his breast, its long, thin arms clutched desperately around his neck.

The woman (Cela Brandini) approaches him.

> CELA BRANDINI
>
> Well. . . ?

> PELLARIN
> (*irritably, as he stops*)
>
> Well, what?

> CELA BRANDINI
>
> That friend of yours is safe now. Aren't you glad?

> PELLARIN
>
> Well . . . sure I am.

> CELA BRANDINI
>
> That monkey's sick.

> PELLARIN
>
> I know — I know.

> CELA BRANDINI
>
> Want me to hold it for you?

> PELLARIN
>
> You wouldn't like it, honey. And she wouldn't let you. It's been like this for the whole trip.

25.   TRAVELING SHOT: as he starts walking and she catches up with him.

> PELLARIN (continued)
>
> How do you mean he's "safe"? — You mean he got away from them?

> CELA BRANDINI
>
> I arranged some help for him. He'll be waiting for you in Madrid . . . Shouldn't we get your monkey some warm milk?

39

PELLARIN

She's already chucked up what I gave her. If it weren't for this stiff breeze — you would have noticed . . . Here comes a boat . . .

CELA BRANDINI

I phoned the yacht. They said that they'd be sending it — I'll ride out with you.

PELLARIN

Cela, honey — I thought our interview was over.

CELA BRANDINI

I'll tell you when it is.

CUT TO:

26. OMITTED

27. SERIES OF SHOTS: (PELLARIN AND CELA IN THE BOAT)

They chug away into the night. The wind is strong, the water choppy.

As she gets to know him better, Cela is finding this man increasingly exasperating, and increasingly attractive.

And she senses some response from him . . . Or is he merely playing with her? . . . He does play with people . . . This, she thinks, is actually a tool for keeping people (even attractive women like herself) at a certain distance.

CELA BRANDINI

That friend of yours is different from the person he pretends to be.

PELLARIN

Old Kim?

CELA BRANDINI

Yes. I've been doing more research —

PELLARIN

Oh, he's *different*. . . .

CELA BRANDINI

I know about the public career, of course—cabinet minister, advisor to three presidents, special envoy—all of that. But I didn't realize his importance academically.

PELLARIN

You've read his books?

CELA BRANDINI

They're difficult—

PELLARIN

And influential.

CELA BRANDINI

He has doctorates in four separate disciplines.

(Good European that she is, she can't help but be impressed by all those doctorates.)

CELA BRANDINI (continued)

And he was your teacher—You must be rather bright yourself. Didn't you finish Harvard magna cum laude?

PELLARIN

He woulda killed me if I hadn't.

She studies him.

CELA BRANDINI

That sounds as though you meant it.

PELLARIN

I always mean it, sugar, I'm a politician.

CELA BRANDINI

Which means that what you'll answer will only *sound* like it's an answer—

PELLARIN

Mainly, what that kinda question means is "Senator—just how dishonest *are* you?" . . . Shall I answer that one? I got married young to the smartest wheeler-dealer in the State of Texas. She sold her pappy's string of painless dental clinics and started in collecting radio and TV stations, junk food

41

franchises and *money* . . . So as a crook, I never had a chance to prove myself.

Cela's sovereign failing is a lack of humor, but this is more than balanced by her powers of intuition.

> CELA BRANDINI
> You're hiding behind jokes . . . Oh, you Americans! Is even honesty a source of guilt? You're all such boring puritans and all so *guilty* . . .

> PELLARIN
> Well, sugar, isn't everybody? So what's wrong with owning up to it? My old grandmother was born into your church. I sometimes envy her —

> BRANDINI
> *(she speaks the word with contempt)*
> Absolution? That's what you're looking for?

He smiles at her.

> PELLARIN
> I don't know yet just *what* I'm looking for. Do you?

> CELA BRANDINI
> It's not my church, Pellarin.

She speaks with a severity bordering on hauteur, and that makes him smile again.

> CELA BRANDINI (continued)
> I'm an anarchist.

> PELLARIN
> I wish you were a veterinarian.

He has never ceased to stroke the little creature's head.

28. FRESH ANGLE

They are drawing nearer to the yacht.

> CELA BRANDINI
> I do not think that monkey has very long to live.

> PELLARIN
> Neither do I.

42

She has been trying again to light her cigarette. But the wind is too much for her.

> CELA BRANDINI
>
> Interesting . . .

> PELLARIN
>
> Death? The subject doesn't capture my imagination.

She stiffens.

> CELA BRANDINI
>
> I know something about it, Pellarin. I've seen it in Vietnam, Central America — in Greece —

> PELLARIN
>
> I know. There's a lot of that stuff going around.

In sudden anger, she throws the cigarette into the sea, then throws her gold lighter after it.

> PELLARIN
>
> Hey! Hold on there —

> CELA BRANDINI
>
> Two months ago I held in my arms, not a monkey, but a dying man. The only one I've ever loved on earth.

This, he understands, was not intended for dramatic effect. Drama is her nature. Of course, she's been trying to impress him, but it is not with her suffering, but her reality as a person. Pellarin, embarrassed, realizes that he has not been treating her as one.

After a silence, she speaks again, this time in a different tone.

> CELA BRANDINI
>
> I was going to say that what I found so interesting was something that I read about your friend. I looked up the famous confession — so-called. He said he'd die first, but that he "would never dare . . ."

> PELLARIN
>
> What's that?

> CELA BRANDINI
>
> To touch . . . to lay a hand on you.

43

Pellarin doesn't speak.

"Never dare" . . . That enormous load of guilt of yours—
doesn't it include your friend?

PELLARIN
(in a voice of stifled anger)
Look, Missy—I didn't write those letters, and they didn't
go to me. You must know that. They all went to a basket
case down in Palm Beach named Vandervanter. And the
whole meghilla got into the hands of somebody's dirty tricks
department —

CELA BRANDINI
Whose?

PELLARIN
Who cares? I'm goddamned if I feel guilty about *that*.

CELA BRANDINI
(coolly)
I'm speaking of the man who wanted you so much, and
didn't dare to touch you with his hands . . . Perhaps he was
afraid . . . you might not help responding . . .

PELLARIN
Shit!

CELA BRANDINI
Well?

PELLARIN
(sharply)
That's . . . not the problem. And it never was.

She cuts him off.

CELA BRANDINI
Or is it that he's impotent? . . .

Interesting that you—a hetero—should have reacted with
such heat to that suggestion.

He looks at her for a moment, with empty eyes.

44

PELLARIN
(*deadpan*)
Golly-gee, Missy, I reckon you already got your second article.

CELA BRANDINI
(*with a certain complacency*)
People tell me more than they intend to.

PELLARIN
Okay! . . . Okay, sugar . . . here's something I'll be glad to tell you — I still love that man.

He has spoken with such perfect simplicity that she accords it a small, respectful silence.

PELLARIN (continued)
I just hope you know the kind of love I mean . . . Or don't you believe that such a thing exists?

She thinks it over . . . fails to find an answer.

He rises as the boat comes alongside the gangway of the yacht.

CELA BRANDINI
(*a trifle sulkily*)
I'll tell you if we ever meet again.

29. FRESH ANGLE

On the gangway he turns back to her.

PELLARIN
Hey — was that thing really gold — a Dunhill?

She looks blank.

PELLARIN (continued)
I'll have one for you . . . when we meet again.

She speaks suddenly:

CELA BRANDINI
Keep clear of the priests, Pellarin. They are the poisoners of great men. Go get yourself a good psychiatrist.

He forces up his famous grin.

45

PELLARIN

The shrinks, honey, don't believe in sin.

CUT TO:

30. EXTERIOR. DECK OF THE YACHT—NIGHT

STRICKLAND

So there you are—!

PELLARIN
(*as he reaches the deck*)

Is there a doctor on this thing?

Strickland has just caught sight of Pellarin's monkey. He backs away a little.

STRICKLAND

Are you contagious?

PELLARIN

The doctor, Garne—where the fuck *is* he?

STRICKLAND

There's no need to shout . . . What *is* that creature?

PELLARIN

Strickland, if I don't get her to the doctor soon, I think she's had it.

STRICKLAND

You don't imagine that a qualified physician like our Dr. Araña is going to deal professionally with some pet ape of yours—

PELLARIN

Sure he's going to. Either that or he gets dropped into the Barcelona harbor.

STRICKLAND
(*pursing his lips*)

Luckily, he's gone ashore. I know, because I *hoped* he might do something helpful with Diana . . .

PELLARIN

What's wrong with *her*?

STRICKLAND

Do you really have to ask?

A brief pause, and an exchange of looks. Then Pellarin starts quickly toward the nearest door.

STRICKLAND
(*calling after him*)

But for God's sake—Don't let her see you now, in *that*
condition—

PELLARIN

I'm looking for the kennels—

STRICKLAND

The *what*?

PELLARIN

Where old Gigi keeps her Afghans, and the fucking pelican
. . . Some kind of steward's got to be in charge of it—

STRICKLAND

The boat deck. Get that thing into a cage, and take a
bath . . .

Pellarin has already gone.

31. THE KENNELS—NIGHT

A melancholy little prison where forgotten creatures squat brooding
in the dark . . . Pellarin finds an empty cage. But the monkey will
not enter it.

PELLARIN
(*in a whisper*)

It's warm enough up here, sugar. Just stay put until I find
a vet—

Terrified, the animal refuses to let go of him.

PELLARIN

Okay, sugar—*okay!* The hell with regulations! Until you're
well, we'll stick together—in my cabin.

47

By now the wretched creature is hysterical, and has begun to dig its sharp claws in his throat.

32. FRESH ANGLE

Struggling, Pellarin moves from the dark cages to the moonlit deck. The monkey's drawing blood—there's no controlling it . . .

Pellarin puts his hands on the long, thin arms, and, using all his strength, yanks them clear.

The monkey, shrieking with fright, makes one great leap into the air. It carries her beyond the rail; and in another instant, Pellarin can hear a tiny splash.

33. FRESH ANGLE

He looks down at the black water . . . Not a sign of her.

His shirt is torn. Raising a hand to close it, he realizes what has happened:

The last thing the monkey had been clinging to had been the necklace—and it's gone into the sea with her.

CUT TO:

34. INTERIOR. CORRIDOR OUTSIDE DIANA'S CABIN—NIGHT

"Garne" Strickland is the self-appointed keeper of one of Washington's best-known secrets: Diana's fondness for the bottle. She is as rigidly discreet about it as her addiction will permit. And Strickland actually enjoys playing nurse to her in those dark hours when nobody must be allowed to see her.

This is such a time. And when the Senator (whom he detests) comes down from the kennels—still unwashed and wild-looking—and starts pounding on the cabin door, Strickland does his gentlemanly best to mute the commotion.

PELLARIN
She's locked it—

STRICKLAND
I should imagine that it's because she wants to be alone.

PELLARIN

Have you a key?

STRICKLAND

I certainly do not.

From inside the cabin there is heard a crash, a tinkle of glass and the unmistakable sound of a falling body.

Pellarin commences throwing his weight against the door. After a violent kick or two, he breaks it open.

35. INTERIOR. THE CABIN

A catastrophic mess . . . Diana, unconscious, is sprawled out on the floor.

STRICKLAND
(*in a hissing whisper*)
We can just thank God they're all ashore . . .

PELLARIN

Get the hell out of there —

It is as if he hadn't spoken. Strickland has brushed past him, and, with a brisk yet gentle movement, is loosening Diana's blouse . . . He takes off her remaining shoe, and makes her comfortable on one of the twin beds.

All Pellarin can do is stand and watch.

Strickland gets some ice out of a champagne bucket and, with a hand towel from the bathroom, begins, with practiced care, to bathe Diana's face.

PELLARIN

Let me do it —

Strickland gives him a basilisk stare.

STRICKLAND

Leave the poor girl alone — !

When Strickland has finished, Pellarin sits down on the other bed . . . Strickland would prefer to get him out of there . . . He stalks to the door, and clicks off all the lights . . . It's evident that Pellarin won't budge.

A pause . . . Then, with a heavy sigh, he stalks away.

Diana stirs a little, murmuring:

> DIANA
>
> Garne . . . ?

> PELLARIN
>
> It's me, sugar . . .

Only the moon illuminates the picture as he sits watching over her.

DISSOLVE:

36.   EXTERIOR. THE AIRPORT IN MADRID — LATE AFTERNOON

Menaker, rather elegantly turned out, is toting his own old bag, as he comes out of the Madrid Airport looking for a cab. He is not pleased when Cela Brandini appears driving a Jeep.

> MENAKER
>
> You're certainly not here by accident.

> CELA BRANDINI
>
> Certainly not.

He hadn't expected her, but he's grateful for the long, cool drink she pours out of a thermos for him.

37.   THE JEEP — STREETS OF MADRID — DAY

> MENAKER
>
> I rather hoped you'd finished with me down in Africa. But here's that damned infernal tape machine of yours again —

> CELA BRANDINI
>
> You really mind?

> MENAKER
>
> I'm bribed with gin, Brandini.

> CELA BRANDINI
>
> Let's get back to the subject —

MENAKER

Blake Pellarin, yes — He really does deserve your generosity —

CELA BRANDINI

And needs it.

MENAKER

Speak of him as he is, "nothing extenuate" . . .
                    (*he chuckles*)
When I remember what you did to poor old Henry —

CELA BRANDINI
                    (*sticking in the banderillas*)
He was always your great rival, wasn't he? Since Harvard days? *And* Washington . . .

MENAKER
                    (*a trifle sharply*)
Rival? . . . As what? Chief brown-noser to the Rockefellers? I wasn't in that race.
            (*he sees that she's enjoying this, and
                quickly shifts to quiet geniality*)
First, I'm a trifle older . . .

CELA BRANDINI

Yes?

MENAKER
                    (*he can't help this*)
And he *is* getting *shorter* — Have you noticed that? He's positively *dwindling* with thwarted ambition: Metternich as the incredible shrinking man. They ought to give poor shrinking Henry one last go at State. As a foreigner, there's no higher he can go — and who knows how much smaller he can get.

CELA BRANDINI

And you?

MENAKER

Another slug of that fine booze, dear Cela — May I call you that? What were you saying?

51

CELA BRANDINI
Secretary of State. If you'd ever had your choice, is that what you'd have settled for?

MENAKER
My hash has been settled for me, Cela. There's no question of choice.

CELA BRANDINI
Some people think you could have gone right to the top.

He considers this for a moment.

MENAKER
I was one of the young people who started under Roosevelt. Some few of us got close enough to catch his interest; and it pleased him to encourage Presidential dreams. It was absurd, of course, but there was one of us who actually made it: Lyndon Johnson.

CELA BRANDINI
But Roosevelt himself would have had another preference —?

MENAKER
(*looking vaguely through the window*)
I'd tell you where to let me off — but I'm not quite certain where I am . . .

CELA BRANDINI
The city's changed.

MENAKER
I hear it's thick in the Prado, the paint is peeling off the Goyas. The smog, I mean . . . And all these banks — My God, how many banks. They all used to be cafes. You wouldn't care too much for banks, I don't suppose. You've mentioned more than once that you're an anarchist.

CELA BRANDINI
My father, too. He died here in the Spanish war.

MENAKER

They were the bravest and the ones you liked the most: a rickety-tickety raggedy-assed crowd of amateurs. The communists, as you know, took charge of that — and then took over. The Kremlin sent in its "advisors" —

CELA BRANDINI
(*with knee-jump anti-Americanism*)
Just like your own "advisors" in Vietnam —

MENAKER
(*ex cathedra*)
History, Miss Brandini, imitates itself, but never quite repeats. Stalin needed to keep Hitler busy for a while, but the last thing he wanted was a Soviet state west of the Pyrenees, so he planned for us to lose — But to lose *slowly*.

CELA BRANDINI
Some place back there I had a question . . .

MENAKER
And you're afraid you'll get another lecture.

CELA BRANDINI
Roosevelt. That's it: his preference for you as a future president —

MENAKER
(*choosing his words*)
Lyndon was a high school teacher from some nowhere place in Texas. Mister Roosevelt might well have been prejudiced just a little —

CELA BRANDINI
In your favor?

MENAKER
Think who he *was*. Of course, he'd lean toward someone with a better brain — from his own culture, his own class . . .
(*he breaks off. Then smiles*)
I see you writing the word "snob" in your invisible notebook.

CELA BRANDINI
Then even if we lay aside the matter of the scandal —

MENAKER
(*cutting her off very sharply*)
If we're laying it aside, why are we bringing it up? . . . Please
ask the car to stop: I'll get off here —

CELA BRANDINI
That's your hotel — ?

MENAKER
I'll wait and see. I think I'd like to take a little walk . . .

38. EXTERIOR. MODEST-LOOKING HOTEL

Menaker, rather cross, descends from the Jeep, gets his bag, and
moves to the hotel door.

She joins him.

CELA BRANDINI
We're all of us some kind of snob. I want to know just how
you would have seen yourself as President.

MENAKER
Truman campaigned by whistle-stop from the back of a
train. Harry was the last. The trains are gone and now our
primaries are two-year marathons, with candidates skipping
about like fleas to catch up with the latest polls. I don't think
you can picture *me* — a man of stout habit and some
dignity — ricocheting through the shopping malls and super-
markets . . . competing with a Nixon, or a Carter, or an
actor — for my own small "television event" on the six-o'clock
news?

CELA BRANDINI
You know what one of your old pupils told me?

MENAKER
(*after a moment*)
I know that pupil.

CELA BRANDINI
He told me you're the greatest man he ever met.

MENAKER
(*in his grandest style*)
If, in my little Harvard garden, some few of the brighter
sprigs felt that about me, it was not an opinion I discour-
aged . . . What truly great ones were they ever likely to en-
counter in this unweeded garden of a world?

CELA BRANDINI
(*leading him on*)
A Socrates without a Plato — ?

MENAKER
Me? I am no Socrates, Madam; and Platos are extinct.

CELA BRANDINI
Samuel Johnson then, without a Boswell?

MENAKER
No, and not Weber without Fields, Smith without Dale, or
even Ozzie without Harriet.

CELA BRANDINI
I am not familiar with those people.

MENAKER
You don't imagine that posterity's judgment, do you?
Posterity is a whim. A shapeless litter of old bones: the mid-
den of a vulgar beast: the most capricious and immense
mass-public of them all — the dead.

CELA BRANDINI
And Pellarin? What will it make of him?

He turns to her. The Augustan air of dignity has ceased to be a jok-
ing affectation. Now he means it.

MENAKER
He'll save our bones, and shield our flesh. He'll be
remembered.

She squints at him through the smoke of her eternal cigarette . . .

There are handicaps, of course. I was just one of them. Harvard was bad enough . . .

He starts up the steps.

55

Good-bye to you, Brandini. I admire you, and hope to God we never meet again.

CELA BRANDINI
What's wrong with Harvard?

He turns again; and here Dr. Menaker's eyes narrow, also, meeting hers.

MENAKER
(*with monumental patience*)
Just too damn far from Texas . . . the Pellarins were all Sam Rayburn's people so, in Washington, it was only natural that Blake should have begun as one of Lyndon's boys . . .

After a pause, he speaks again, with quiet pride.

But he was really, of course, one of mine . . . the best of them.

CELA BRANDINI
(*with a kind of coy, and not unfriendly, malice*)
You've spoken of his limitations—What are yours?

He is very tired.

MENAKER
I'm an old man, Miss Brandini—and a faggot. I couldn't use another limitation.

39. OMITTED

40. EXTERIOR. THE RAMBLAS IN BARCELONA—DAY

At the roundpoint near the foot of this great boulevard there stands one of the largest and gaudiest of the great cinema palaces in Catalonia. A taxi hustles up and stops at the entrance, and Sheldon Buckle leaps nimbly out of it. A quick look to right and left, and then he darts into the movie theatre, stopping abruptly just inside the entrance to observe—

41. INTERIOR. FOYER OF THE MOVIE HOUSE.

An excited group of foreign gentlemen in rumpled but expensive-looking suits are gathered here . . . It seems (to Dinty Benart, especially) an odd hour of the morning for movie-going, but the eleven-thirty showing is an institution in this popular house, and what with the crowd around the box office and the language barrier, the whole business is hot and tiresome, and shortens tempers among the Pellarin advisors.

KINZEL
(*in a hoarse and angry half-whisper*)
The man's a *pro*, I tell you—

STRICKLAND
The man's a certifiable lunatic—!

Dinty Benart has the tickets. He waves them high, signaling them in—

Between velvet curtains there can be glimpsed a peculiarly bad Iberian film production in the sentimental vein.

41A. THE AUDITORIUM

KINZEL
(*as they take seats in the almost-empty theatre*)
Listen, I was Goddamn lucky to bump into him—

DINTY
But did you have to drag us here to see a *movie*—a *Spanish* movie?

KINZEL
Security. The media's all over town. Look at Brandini. If we were *seen* together—

DINTY
Brandini's gone.

STRICKLAND
(*sharply*)
Where to?

DINTY
Madrid. Anyway, what's wrong with a hotel?

STRICKLAND
I'd dearly love one, but it's the tourist season, and they come in packages. Blake got the last bed in the country.

57

DINTY

The Hotel Palace in Madrid.

KINZEL

I *see* . . .

Actually, he doesn't see a thing. Not even the mustachioed character who now looms over them.

BUCKLE

Good morning, gentlemen.

Startled, Kinzel almost jumps out of his shoes. But quickly recovers.

KINZEL

Buckle! Hi, there . . . didn't see you coming in—

BUCKLE
(*deadly quiet in his complacency*)

Naturally.

Dinty stares at him, incredulous and horrified.

DINTY

Buckle?!

BUCKLE
(*with air of taking over the meeting*)

J. Sheldon Buckle. By way of presenting my credentials, allow me to present you with some information. According to my brief from Mr. Kinzel, you gentlemen are interested in a man (if "man" should be used for such a creature) traveling under the name of Menaker—

DINTY
(*unimpressed*)

What about him?

BUCKLE
(*with a certain quiet triumph*)

I'll tell you were you'll find that man—in Africa.

58

STRICKLAND
(*sweetly, after a brief pause*)
Mr. Buckle, I have a maiden aunt in Philadelphia who happens to be very deaf. We might cable her. It's barely possible she hasn't heard that news.

Buckle rigidly disregards this last.

BUCKLE
In the Republic of Batunga, Menaker has been retained — *de*tained may be the word for it by now — in the matter of some ivory . . .

DINTY
Who gives a shit?

BUCKLE
(*unruffled, continues*)
This Menaker uncovered a gross excess of it, and has been rash enough to publicly denounce the illegality of a mass slaughter of the elephant —

STRICKLAND
Buckle —

BUCKLE
Yes?

STRICKLAND
I was just going to tell you to shut up.

On the big screen the bad movie continues.

BUCKLE
I have a point to make —

DINTY
Then get to it.

BUCKLE
This Menaker is an acute embarrassment — not only to you gentlemen, but to the actual owner of the ivory: the Field Marshal Mgobo, with whom I am on confidential terms. So . . .

59

DINTY
So what?

BUCKLE
(*in lowered tones*)
If you should happen to be thinking — well . . . what I'm thinking . . .

Nobody wants a glimpse into his thoughts . . .

Jerry Kinzel (Buckle's patron) is severe:

KINZEL
We want to keep the man *away*, that's *all*. There's no question of "termination with prejudice," understand?

BUCKLE
The phrase is out of style. You'll only find it in the spy stories.

STRICKLAND
Well — ! That's something to be grateful for.

BUCKLE
Now it's XPD.

KINZEL
XPD?

DINTY
What's that?

BUCKLE
Expedient demise.

After which triumphant piece of one-upmanship, Buckle — before anyone can stop him — exits.

42.   FRESH ANGLE

At the far side of a candy vending machine, Buckle pauses, listening . . . He hears:

DINTY'S VOICE
I don't know about the rest of you, but I don't want to see this movie —

A low grumble of assent from the others.

DINTY'S VOICE (continued)
Tell you what *I* think — I think we're going to Madrid.

A glitter enters the dark eyes of Sheldon Buckle . . . The game's afoot
. . . He hastens away to book his space on the first plane.

CUT TO:

43. INTERIOR. THE HOTEL PALACE IN MADRID — DAY

Pellarin arrives; is graciously welcomed at the doorway. There's a
message for the distinguished Senator . . . Pellarin opens the
envelope, but before he can read it, the *conserje* stops him with some
news: Mrs. Pellarin has phoned to say that she'll be flying up from
Barcelona to join him: arriving in the late afternoon. And what about
the Senator's luggage?

PELLARIN
Send it up, thank you — I'm late for an appointment.

44. EXTERIOR. PALACE HOTEL — DAY

Waiting for the taxi, he opens the envelope and reads the message:

> "Cafe 'Los Tres Hermanos'
> (former coffee house)
> Calle Mejias Blanco, 18.
> Two o'clock. Be prompt.
>
> Signed: Mother Machree."

Pellarin crumples the note and gets into the cab, which pulls away.

45. DOWN SHOT

As Pellarin's taxi hustles up the street, the crumpled message is tossed
out from the window . . . A second taxi, not far behind, comes to
a sudden grinding halt. The figure of a man is seen to leap nimbly
out, scurry through traffic, and retrieve the piece of paper . . .

CUT TO:

46. INTERIOR. THE CAFE: "LOS TRES HERMANOS" — MADRID —
DAY

Obviously Senator Pellarin could not be seen with Kimball Menaker
in any public place where they'd be likely to be recognized. This was
Menaker's choice.

61

When Pellarin arrives by cab, he finds his old friend at a table by the window.

                    MENAKER
     You're late.

                    PELLARIN
     I know. I'm sorry. Also thanks for taking all this trouble.
     What are we drinking?

                    MENAKER
     I've been drinking wine.
                    (*he raises his glass*)
     Good, cheap *clarete*. Haven't had any for forty years.

He turns to the waiter-bartender, asking for another glass.

                    PELLARIN
     It's all that time since you've been in Madrid? Then . . . what
     about the fence?

                    MENAKER
     Fence . . . ?

                    PELLARIN
     You knew him somewhere else, I guess —

He breaks off as the glass comes to the table. Menaker fills it from a small stone pitcher.

                    PELLARIN (continued)
                    (*a bit impatiently*)
     So what's he offering?

                    MENAKER
     Well, stolen property, you know. You'll have to figure on
     a big discount —

He stops, noticing that Pellarin is strangely silent — He's peering intently through the window.

                    PELLARIN
     You see that man out there —

Menaker looks.

                    62

47. FRESH ANGLE

The street, in the bright dazzle of the afternoon sun, seems empty.
But Menaker can see the car parked on the corner in the shade.
Behind the wheel a dark young man sits waiting.

48. BACK TO SCENE:

                    MENAKER
The rough trade in the Citroen?

                    PELLARIN
He calls himself her brother. It could be he's her pimp.

                    MENAKER
The Brazilian manicurist? What's he waiting for?

                    PELLARIN
The money, I suppose.

                    MENAKER
He's rather fetching. Bring him in. I'd like to see the man's
. . . credentials — among other things.

                    PELLARIN
Kim, I wish you wouldn't . . .

He breaks off, reluctant to continue.

                    MENAKER
Wouldn't what?

                    PELLARIN
Well — camp around like that.

                    MENAKER
So do I. It tends to grow on one. I made such a noisy bang
when I was finally dragged out of the closet, that ever since
a certain . . . self-consciousness seems to urge me on to these
bad jokes about it.

                    PELLARIN
                 (suddenly angry)
You didn't have to resign! Not these days, for Chrissake!
Not from *Harvard* —

63

MENAKER
Not just because I was in love, you mean?

PELLARIN
You didn't have to give up your professorship.

MENAKER
In love with one of my own students — with a boy?

PELLARIN
Who would have ever known? God knows *I* didn't. Besides,
twenty years ago . . .

MENAKER
In the closet it was more like forty. That's quite a stretch
in solitary. Now I'm out I rather find I like it . . . Out in
the sunlight, under the moon; lovely young dancers and the
sound of flutes. I like it very much.

Silence. Then, with a change of tone:

MENAKER (continued)
That gloomy little treat out there — is he a blackmailer?

PELLARIN
He doesn't know about *Diana* — just what I promised *Tina*.

MENAKER
Ah! Then we're dealing, are we, with a *promise*? You're still
pretending that the girl would get in trouble if she tried to
fence the stuff herself? And still assuming she's a jewel
robber —

PELLARIN
Since I've seen you, I'm afraid that situation is more
complicated . . .

MENAKER
(*incredulous*)
Don't tell me you've returned the emeralds to your wife?

PELLARIN
I . . . I can't —

64

MENAKER

You must tell me all about it when I'm back —

He starts toward the door.

PELLARIN

Back from where?

MENAKER
(*on his way to the door*)
You might be recognized.

Blake asks if there's a telephone. There is, and he calls up the Ritz.

PELLARIN

Senator Pellarin here, may I speak please to Mrs. Pellarin — ?
That is, if she's arrived . . .

He watches through the window as Menaker approaches the car and falls into a lively conversation with the young man at the wheel.

A pause.

PELLARIN

She doesn't answer . . . Thank you.

He hangs up.

49.   MENAKER RETURNS

PELLARIN

Well — ? What did he say?

MENAKER
(*sitting down*)
We made an appointment.
(*dropping his voice*)
There's someone else, though — just beyond those trees. Do you recall a gentleman named Buckle?

PELLARIN

Old J. Sheldon? He was in the Nixon mob.

MENAKER

But not among those present at the Watergate, and that's the tragedy of Sheldon's life. Perhaps the poor crazed thing

65

has failed some mission, and is . . . He keeps on doing that, you know. Failing and waiting. Don't fret, Boysie. I'll give him an evasive answer.

PELLARIN

Okay — back to business. You *have* seen the fence — ?

MENAKER

Well, the insurance people pay the best. But then you couldn't go to them.

PELLARIN

I guess *you* couldn't either . . . What would you tell them?

MENAKER

I know what they'd tell *me*. You seem to have forgotten that the necklace hasn't been insured.

PELLARIN

What makes you think that?

A blank silence.

MENAKER

I have forgotten that.

PELLARIN

You have forgotten why we're in Madrid? *You* named the town. Now name the price.

MENAKER

We'll need the necklace to do that.

PELLARIN

Sixty thousand dollars — that's what it's really worth.

MENAKER

I think you'd better have a talk about that with your wife.

PELLARIN

That would be quite some conversation.

MENAKER

Not if you give it back to her.

PELLARIN

I can't do that . . . The monkey took it.

Menaker stares at him.

MENAKER

Where did he take it *to*?

PELLARIN

The monkey died.

MENAKER

I was afraid of that. I assume there was a simple burial at sea.

He breaks off, suddenly guessing the truth, and trying not to laugh.

PELLARIN

Yes. There was a last convulsion and they both went overboard.

MENAKER

So what we're looking for is a receiver for some stolen goods that don't exist.

PELLARIN

Goddamn it, Kim, I want an *estimate*, that's all—*You* sit there looking cute and cryptic—

MENAKER

Don't I just.

PELLARIN

Let's have the truth: I bet you haven't even *seen* that fence.

MENAKER

The truth, dear boy . . . well, sixty thousand? That was the price mentioned by your wife?

PELLARIN

Constantly.

MENAKER

When you ran for Congress that first time . . .

Menaker holds his eye in silence for a moment.

MENAKER (continued)
Did you ever ask yourself how you got in?

PELLARIN
I always thought we ran a pretty good campaign.

MENAKER
An expensive one. Diana's father was expected to provide
the main financing. But then you quarreled with the old
bustard over some splendid point of principle, and he backed
away . . .

PELLARIN
That's true.

MENAKER
It's also true Diana was the one who bought you all those
extra spots on radio. Now, can you guess where she got all
that money from?

Pellarin looks aghast.

PELLARIN
She sold the emeralds — ?
                    (*Menaker nods*)
Oh, my God!

MENAKER
And ever afterwards, my beamish boy — her famous
emeralds were paste.

PELLARIN
My *God* — !

MENAKER
You keep on saying that. We all have our little whims. You
are, sporadically, a lunatic — and try to hide it. I, on the
other hand, like showing off. I must confess that I've been
doing that just now. And also leading you — from
Batunga — slightly down the garden path.

PELLARIN
How do you mean?

MENAKER

We'll get to that this evening. For now, the girl was promised money, and her brother thinks it would be nice for her
to have it.

Pellarin has risen.

MENAKER

You're going—?

PELLARIN

I've got to get it, don't I?

MENAKER

Well, old darling, not a really *gross* amount. That would
mean trouble all around.

PELLARIN

Diana, too . . .

MENAKER
(sharply)

Diana, *what*—? You're also giving money to your *wife*?

PELLARIN

It's not to make up for what I took from her—It's . . .

The old man's face is flushed with sudden anger:

MENAKER

What she gave to *you*? She gave you nothing! She's only
driven you to where *she* wants to go—
*(he stops and tries to
pull himself together)*
I know—you think I'm prejudiced. But why should you feel
guilty? About her—*or* your Goddamn manicurist?

PELLARIN

Or about you—? I have guilt enough to go around.

Kim Menaker gives him a sudden, steady look.

MENAKER

We've had our compensations.

Pellarin meets his look, and smiles at him with real affection.

69

PELLARIN

But you *are* prejudiced.

MENAKER

Of course I am. She's lusted for the White House all these
years — forget her string of paste, and give her that.

DISSOLVE:

50.   INTERIOR. A SMALL SEAFOOD BAR — DAY

On one of the more dubious side streets near the Gran Via . . . A
dubious establishment, as Strickland is the first to point out.

STAN LOEB is the newcomer in their group.

LOEB

This is the kind of joint the cops are always watching.

DINTY

So what are we doing here?

STRICKLAND

We'll have to wait for Jerry

Aside from his rather special relationship with Diana, Garne
Strickland occupies, in the high-priced galaxy of Pellarin satellites,
an official post of some importance. He is the senior partner, company wasp, and original financier of the prestigious firm of Pellarin,
Loeb, Leibowitz and Cirello: image makers. Clients include rock
superstars, trial lawyers, Beverly Hills plastic surgeons and TV
evangelists . . . It had been thought that, in sending Strickland on
the yachting party, a useful function had been found for him at last.

But now Stan Loeb is here . . .

LOEB

So what's with Barcelona?

DINTY

The yacht —

LOEB
(*cutting him off*)
When I heard Madrid, right away I thought of whatsis —
that international thing that's going on —

70

                    STRICKLAND
and on and on.

                       LOEB
"INTERCOM" — that's it. The whole schamozzle's sillier than
bingo.

                      DINTY
                    (*sighing*)
All the same it's where we ought to have him now.

                       LOEB
Madrid?

                      DINTY
Maybe a network interview — "An optimistic look ahead — "

                    STRICKLAND
He'll never play it right. We'd get that well-known
sarcasm . . .

                      DINTY
But look at the exposure: the whole fuckin' world is there:
the Ruskies, and the Goddamn French —

                       LOEB
So why did he come *here*?

                    STRICKLAND
Who knows? We can't even *find* him —

            A DEEP, PENETRATING VOICE
I have . . . I've found him.

Stan Loeb emits a long, despairing groan.

                       LOEB
Buckle! — Who let *you* in?

All turn as Sheldon Buckle materializes out of the gloom.

                      BUCKLE
This town has always been a great recruiting base. I've signed
up many a good man right in this little bar.

                        71

LOEB

Where's Jerry?

BUCKLE

Kinzel? I got him to spell for me awhile, so's I could come
here and consult with you. He's at the Banco de Bilboa, keeping an eye on Pellarin.

LOEB

What's he doing in a *bank*?

STRICKLAND

Cashing a traveler's check, perhaps, or in a secret conclave
with Karl Malden —

LOEB

Buckle —

BUCKLE

Yes, Mr. Loeb?

LOEB

Show us your palm.

Buckle does so. The palm and fingers are deeply, and disgustingly
scarred.

LOEB

Thank you, Buckle, that's enough.

BUCKLE

First — given your permission — I'll pass on my news.

He pauses for effect.

STRICKLAND

Well, then, get on with it. We wouldn't want to keep you
a moment longer than is necessary.

Buckle moves closer to the group, dropping his voice to a hoarse
whisper.

BUCKLE

Kimball Menaker . . .

STRICKLAND

We know all that: it happened that the Senator ran into him
someplace in Africa —

BUCKLE

Menaker is here, gentlemen — at least he's in Madrid — And
very obviously, by appointment . . .

Having created the sensation he'd been looking forward to, Buckle
nods curtly and strides out of the restaurant.

STRICKLAND
(after a numb silence)
Jee-zus! Now what do we do?

DINTY

Hey — what about that scar? He was in Nam, I guess —

LOEB

Buckle? He's been in lots of places where there's trouble. I
don't know where they had the waffle iron. But it was Buckle
who turned on the heat, and put his hand on it — and kept
it there. Dinty, you get that lousy, fuckin' schlemiel's ass
out of the country, and I hope you hear me good.

DINTY

How?

LOEB

That's your problem.

STRICKLAND

And Menaker? Whose problem is that? . . .

A pause.

Nobody has any answer.

51.   EXTERIOR. THE RETIRO, THE GREAT PARK IN MADRID —
(LATE AFTERNOON)

For their second meeting place, Menaker has chosen this very public
place, as being probably the least infected with American tourists.

After some searching, Blake locates Menaker behind a bush.

73

PELLARIN

Aren't you carrying this thing a little far — ? Hiding like this,
I mean — in the bushes?

MENAKER

Not *hiding*, you fat-headed young fool . . . But keep your
voice down anyway . . .

Pellarin looks around.

MENAKER (continued)

And what the hell have you got there? a briefcase, like a
bloody bureaucrat?

PELLARIN

What *are* you doing?

MENAKER

I've been looking at that boy.

A young Spaniard, pale and terribly thin, and dressed in tatters, lies
sleeping on a bench. Now Pellarin notices what Menaker has been
watching.

PELLARIN
(*disgusted*)

Kim — !

MENAKER

Shut up! . . .
(*after a pause*)
You really want to know?

PELLARIN

I asked the question.

MENAKER

You take me for a dirty old man spying on little children
in the park? He looks like Vanni . . .

Pause.

PELLARIN
(*coldly*)

Oh?

74

MENAKER

Oh, yes, my little Vanni used to look like that . . . as rag-
gedy and poor as that. It was his military uniform.

PELLARIN

You actually fought in Spain together, you two?

MENAKER

I only came to be with him. He only came to die.

PELLARIN

He didn't, though . . .

MENAKER

Not quite. That was another of his failures.

PELLARIN

And I'm another one of yours.

MENAKER

Ah, no, Boysie. You're still riding on that carousel. Up and
down with all the music playing. Who knows? Next time
around you'll catch the big brass ring.

A pause, filled only with the distant cries of children at their games.

MENAKER (continued)

He caught it not so far from here . . . And when they'd just
as good as killed him, I finally realized that I'd . . . never
given him enough. And so I . . . I tried to make him laugh.
That's how the letters happened—at the start. It was all that
I could do for that half-creature down in Florida strapped
up into that wheelchair . . .

Music: In another part of the Retiro, a band concert has commenced.

MENAKER (continued)

Better to die on your feet than to live on and on and on
for forty empty years, able to move three fingers, and to
drool . . .

There's always, as you know, the lover and the loved . . .
If Vanni *was* the lover, he didn't . . . make me . . . anything
I wasn't born to be. He taught me—tenderness. And

75

sometimes we would make each other laugh. That's what
I liked about him, really.

During this next, Menaker is very careful to avoid looking Pellarin
in the eye.

Years later when *I* fell in love—hopelessly—I started writing
Vanni about that. Somewhere, inside that mummy filled
with pain,I hoped to make him laugh at me . . .

Or some damned thing . . .

Both men are suddenly engulfed in a wave of mutual embarrassment
. . . To cover this and change the mood, Blake takes out a little key
and unlocks his briefcase.

It is neatly and completely filled with paper money.

> MENAKER (continued)
> Good sweet creeping Jesus! That must be every last peseta
> in the country.

> PELLARIN
> It wasn't easy raising it this quickly, and in cash . . .
>
> You've seen the brother—if that's what he is?

> MENAKER
> That's what he is: your regulation Latin brother seething
> with wild concern for the honor of his little Tina.

> PELLARIN
> Fuck his little Tina.

> MENAKER
> Putting it succinctly, that's just what he's afraid of. He came
> to visit her all the way from someplace I've forgotten, and
> they won't let her off the boat.

> PELLARIN
> What? They didn't tell me that—

> MENAKER
> They never tell you anything . . . Shore leave denied till they
> can get her to Brazil. The poor thing's scared of their police,
> and I don't blame her. The brother thinks we're gibbering
> maniacs, and personally, I think he's right.

Menaker's eyes are still glued on the open briefcase.

MENAKER (continued)
And you propose to pay that . . . that *fortune* to some fingernail polisher, just because it might just possibly have crossed her tiny mind to steal a string of paste?

PELLARIN
That's what I thought I'd sort of given her . . . What do you think the fake ones cost Diana?

MENAKER
Figure the setting—back in those days: three thousand at the most.

PELLARIN
Good. Let's count it out—

And now begins the slow and laborious exchange of money, from one man to another. This curious, almost surreal transaction proceeds during a great part of the following.

MENAKER
And the difference? Who's going to get all that—?

PELLARIN
(*a bit surprised the question should be asked*)
Diana—naturally.

MENAKER
(*a bit cross at the reply*)
The junk-food queen? She owns half of Texas.

PELLARIN
I've just learned what she did for me. She never even mentioned it. That makes me quite some kind of a shit, wouldn't you say?

MENAKER
Well, if all you want is to buy back a little self-esteem, you've got a bargain—

PELLARIN
. . . No, all I'll buy is something pretty for her, and keep my trap shut.

MENAKER
And all this that I'm getting now?

PELLARIN
Didn't you arrange to see that mother-fucking brother?

MENAKER
I'm meeting him an hour from now. America, America—!
We feel bad about something and our first thought is to kiss
it and make it well with money . . .

Pellarin, very ill-tempered, resumes his counting. Obviously, he hates
doing it now . . .

MENAKER (continued)
(*not kindly*)
It's your mazoola, buster-boy.

Before Pellarin snaps it shut, Menaker can see that the briefcase is
still full of money.

MENAKER
That was a short count.

PELLARIN
(*boiling quietly*)
Damn right it is.

MENAKER
How *did* you get your hands on all of that?

PELLARIN
I know some people here in banking—

MENAKER
I don't; so what am I supposed to do with what you've given
me?

PELLARIN
Keep it in your pocket.

MENAKER
It'll never fit . . .

PELLARIN

Pockets, plural — Spread it out all over you.

Menaker, not pleased, starts stuffing money into various parts of his ample person.

Pellarin has turned away. He's looking at the sleeping boy . . . The patched-up shoes are placed very neatly on the pathway just below his head.

PELLARIN

Poor little bastard, he hasn't any socks.

In the distance the brass band finishes, and there's a melancholy smattering of applause . . .

MENAKER
(*still busy stowing*)

In Vanni's brigade they only had a rinky-dink old rifle from the First World War. One for every three men. They'd trade it off between them, and every morning they'd all go to battle — two men out of three without a weapon.

Pause.

That was how I found him . . . one night, sleeping on a bench . . . like that . . .

52. DOLLY SHOT:

On a sudden, rather angry impulse, Blake walks over and stuffs some paper money in one of the boy's shoes.

Old Kim watches this . . . Then, after a moment, joins him: putting money of his own into the other shoe.

These gestures are made with a certain formality, like lighting candles in a church.

Then both retreat.

MENAKER
(*after a moment*)

Perhaps we should have wakened him.

PELLARIN

So he could thank us?

79

MENAKER

Don't be an ass. I'm thinking of the wind.

PELLARIN

I haven't noticed any.

CAMERA FOLLOWS as they move away a little farther, sitting down together on the lip of an old fountain.

PELLARIN

We've never talked about him . . . about your Vanni.

MENAKER

He was worse than you are — lazier . . .

That's quite a lot of money we left there —

Pause.

53.   FRESH ANGLE

Kim Menaker has risen, his back turned to Blake, and moved a step or so away.

MENAKER

I was ahead of him in school, but he was older; so of course, people said that *he* corrupted *me* . . .
            (*a short bark of laughter*)
Here in Spain we were just two frightened Anglos — our clumsy little gropings would be a laughing stock in any gay community today . . .

The wind *is* starting up —

Silence.

What would you say if all the money blows away?

PELLARIN

Symbolic — that's what I'd say. Disgustingly symbolic . . .
Let's just wait and see what happens.

Another silence.

PELLARIN

Tell me about Spain.

MENAKER

This was the first city that was ever bombed. And how the world was shocked. In those days we were innocent. We still believed mass murder from the skies was quite a sin.

But in Madrid in those days the children made a game of it. And sang a song out of a Disney short —

"Quiene tiene miedo del tri-mo-tor — tri-mo-tor" . . .

That was the Caprioni, with three motors — who was afraid of that?

They'd hold hands in a circle, dancing, and when the song was over they'd shout: "Yo! — Me — I'm scared of it!" And the sirens would be screaming, and they'd scatter, laughing . . .

After a moment, Pellarin rises. Then stops himself from moving.

PELLARIN

I guess we'd better wait . . .

MENAKER
(absently)

Wait for what?

PELLARIN

The money in his shoes . . . Somebody might come along and steal it.

Distantly, the band strikes up another tune.

54. FRESH ANGLE

Menaker's voice suddenly changes when he speaks again:

MENAKER

On a sunny morning early in November, the people woke up in this city and discovered that they had no government. All through the night the whole government of their Republic had gone tiptoeing away to safety in the South.

Before we knew it, Franco's Foreign Legionnaires and howling Mussulmans were right here in the outskirts of Madrid.

You could take a streetcar to the front line. But not the subway—On the subway you could end up on the wrong side.

                    PELLARIN
You were lucky, Kim.

                    MENAKER
Lucky?

                    PELLARIN
You got to fight the good one.

                    MENAKER
We lost it. The purpose is to win. And anyway, I didn't fight. I sat in the Gran Via Hotel, and waited for my Vanni . . .
                    (*he turns to Blake to look*
                      more closely at him)
I think you're sulking just a bit.

55.   FRESH ANGLE

                    PELLARIN
Not at all.

                    MENAKER
Brooding, then.

Even the purest "straight" can feel a tiny pang of jealousy.

                    PELLARIN
I was just thinking of your friend.

                    MENAKER
I was waiting for him when he caught it—Safe in the Gran Via Hotel where everybody stayed: Malraux, Ehrenberg, Dos Passos . . . Hemingway wasn't there that year.

I came with Haldane—snuck in as some kind of expert on I don't know what—expected to have answers to I don't know what. That's how I got myself a room in the Gran Via . . . And when he could, he'd come back from the wars, and spend the night with me . . . My little blue-eyed soldier boy . . .

His army was a ragtag crowd of amateurs, ridiculously brave . . . But when the big guns got *too* big, they ran away like rabbits.

But then one day, it happened.

The rabbits suddenly stood up again like lions, and this whole city with them. And they stopped Franco dead.

The streets were full of corpses — little corpses: the children who had sung that song about the tri-mo-tor. The sky was noisy and belonged to death. But there was gold dust in the air.

It was the great November . . .

Hemingway wasn't there, but I was.

56. FRESH ANGLE

PELLARIN
Look who's coming . . .

57. FRESH ANGLE

Three big, tough-looking sailors, wearing their uniforms with a certain menacing panache, are walking up the path in the direction of the sleeping boy.

MENAKER
(*anxiously*)
They'll see it — the money — they can't miss it.

PELLARIN
Easy come — easy go.

MENAKER
You're going to just stand by and let them do it — ?

PELLARIN
Look at the big one: he can beat the living shit out of us both.

58. FRESH ANGLE

One of the three nudges another, then all come to a halt in front of the shoes. They look quickly around, then put their heads together in earnest, whispered conversation. It seems clear that they are either discussing how this unexpected treasure is to be divided between them, or in which direction they should run away with it.

59.   INTERCUT

Then, as Pellarin and Menaker look on in amazement, the "big one" moves behind the bench and, looming over it, taps the boy gently and rather tentatively on the shoulder.

The boy wakes and looks up at the three huge, intimidating figures surrounding him . . . They point to his shoes all stuffed with money. The boy looks, then shakes his head. No (he's saying), that money couldn't possibly be his . . . As for the fearsome sailors — they are protesting that it certainly isn't *theirs.*

So, then, whose *is* it?

All four look about them in bewilderment (Pellarin and Menaker taking care to remain well-hidden).

The sailors are now carefully emptying the shoes, and helping the boy to put them on . . . Then they offer him the money. He shakes his head emphatically. For a moment it's a standoff.

"If it isn't *your* money," they're saying, "it surely isn't ours, either — so it's nobody's."

All think this over for a moment.

Suddenly the big one claps a tremendous buffet on the boy's thin shoulders.

"But they *are* your shoes . . . Well, then — what's in your shoes is yours to keep! But next time you take a nap, don't be a little donkey and leave a great fortune out under the sky like that for anyone to grab. This is a crooked world, remember."

They sally away very cheerfully . . .

The boy — still more bewildered than overjoyed — stuffs the big wad of pesetas in his ragged clothes as best he can, and hurries off.

Menaker is delighted.

MENAKER
Now where on earth could that happen except here in this dumb country?

The band music sounds brighter now.

60. TRAVELING SHOT: Menaker starts walking, Pellarin joining him.

> PELLARIN
> I guess you're glad you came . . .

> MENAKER
> (speaking grumpily, hiding his pleasure)
> Mixed emotions. May I ask a favor?

> PELLARIN
> Go ahead.

> MENAKER
> We'll both be gone tomorrow—I don't know where. Give
> me tonight . . . Join me for dinner.

A slight, rather tense little pause.

> PELLARIN
> You know I *want* to . . .

> MENAKER
> (with a bitter smile)
> But you can't . . .
> (he makes a guess)
> because your wife is here.

> PELLARIN
> She came specially—

> MENAKER
> So did I.

He brings out from his pocket something wrapped in tissue paper.

> MENAKER
> She's got you for life. But you know, Boysie, I think I have
> some rather potent competition.

He shows him the small package, but doesn't open it. He starts to
walk again, Blake at his side.

> MENAKER (continued)
> But tell me something first: —Is there anything still left in
> the whole wide world you truly care about?

PELLARIN

I can make a damn good guess at what you want to hear
me tell you.

MENAKER

Have a try.

PELLARIN

My . . . obligations?

MENAKER
(*suddenly*)
Your duties to your own God-given gifts . . .
(*change of tone*)
You've heard that lecture. Just tell me, present company ex-
cepted, who you care about . . . *Or* if you *can* still care at
all.

PELLARIN

A stupid question.

MENAKER

Answer the stupid question.

Silence . . . Then Menaker throws him a half-whispered clue.

Paris.

Pellarin turns very pale.

PELLARIN
(*after another silence*)
Christ only knows I was in love with her . . . You *ought*
to know.
(*sharply*)
Why dig *that* up?

MENAKER

You were in love with her . . . Love, Senator? What happens when that happens?

PELLARIN

Spare me the metaphysics.

MENAKER

We discover that we're suddenly . . . someone else.

61. TRAVELING SHOT

Menaker starts walking again—leading Pellarin.

> MENAKER
>
> Even the great ones must have sometimes felt uncomfortable in their own skins. Caesar must have dreamt of Alexander, and Napoleon of Caesar—

> PELLARIN
>
> Shit, Professor—I couldn't make their weight.

> MENAKER
>
> Then think of poor Dick Nixon—mincing about inside his fortress in the Oval Room, all bristling with bugs—hoping a playback would eventually inform him who he was . . . He told us often what he *wasn't*, but he never really got it figured out.

Pellarin stops.

> PELLARIN
>
> Neither have I . . . You sly old son of a bitch, so *that's* what you've been getting at.

Menaker sinks down on a bench.

> MENAKER
>
> In a perfect world, all of us should be allowed some short vacations from our own identities. Last week you were Bulldog Drummond, gentleman jewel thief. Soon you'll be hoping to sneak down that rabbit hole again to where it's always Paris in the spring . . .

> PELLARIN
>
> You came sneaking down that rabbit hole yourself.

> MENAKER
>
> Not sneaking—panting like a wounded hart. That rabbit hole of yours was some damned student's ghetto in the Latin Quarter—six flights up.

> PELLARIN
>
> Just four—

MENAKER

It seemed like ten. It almost killed me.

PELLARIN

19A the rue Jacob.

MENAKER

And naturally, you'll tell me it was the happiest time in all your life.

PELLARIN

I was getting a late start . . . I was learning to be young . . . You hadn't given me much time for that.

MENAKER

The woman left you.

There was something a little mean in Menaker's voice; and something dangerous in the look Pellarin now flashes him.

PELLARIN

She had my letter, Kim . . . You gave it to her . . .

Menaker doesn't speak.

PELLARIN (continued)

And yet . . . when I came back there, she was gone . . .

Silence again.

PELLARIN (continued)

I spent a fortune looking for her.

MENAKER

Private detectives, yes. I shouldn't think she'd care too much for that.

Menaker raises the small object wrapped in tissue paper.

MENAKER (continued)

Do you still dream of finding her?

With slow, teasing gestures he unwraps his little package.

MENAKER (continued)

What would you give me if I made the dream come true?

PELLARIN

Christ — ?

A woman's gold ring is revealed, with a big, fine ruby.

MENAKER

Take it.

PELLARIN

It's not the same one . . .

MENAKER

Oh, but it *is*.

Pellarin stares at him.

PELLARIN

The same ring that I gave to her? . . . How the hell did *you* get hold of it?

MENAKER

She threw it at me.

PELLARIN

When was that?

MENAKER

After she'd read your letter.

A pause.

In Menaker's eyes there is a gleam of something not benevolent — almost devilish.

MENAKER (continued)

She's here, Boysie . . . In Madrid. She really is.

Pellarin stares at him . . .

DISSOLVE:

62. INTERIOR. THE HOTEL PALACE — THE PELLARINS' SUITE — EVENING

Enter Pellarin.

DIANA

Take off your trousers.

PELLARIN
(*who has just come in*)
Why?

DIANA
They look as though you had been sleeping in them.

Absently he unbuttons and steps out of his pants. She picks them up and automatically searches the pockets.

DIANA
Aren't you going to take a shower at least?

PELLARIN'S VOICE (offscreen)
(*from the bathroom*)
No time. Didn't I tell you?

DIANA
You haven't told me anything. You never do . . . I don't know why I *came* here—

PELLARIN'S VOICE (offscreen)
Neither do I.

Sudden tears start into her eyes.

PELLARIN'S VOICE (offscreen, continued)
I'm just here overnight. *And* I'll be busy. You should have stayed in Barcelona.

DIANA
I came with that Brandini woman. She's dining with us.

PELLARIN'S VOICE (offscreen)
Tonight? I need to see some people.

DIANA
I booked our table. She has an eye out for you, as I'm sure you've noticed . . . And I thought—

She breaks off.

Emptying the last of his pockets she finds something . . .

He has been shaving and comes out of the bathroom now, patting his cheeks and hurriedly dousing himself with cologne. Reaching for a shirt, he's arrested by his wife's reflection in the mirror. Her freshly made-up face streaming with tears.

90

PELLARIN

Oh, my God—*Sugar!*

He tries to take her in his arms. She pulls away.

You've got it wrong. I don't give a damn for that Italian woman—

DIANA

I know you don't.

PELLARIN

Well, then—?

She opens her clenched fist, showing him . . . the ring.

He draws in a deep breath of air, and sits down on the edge of the bed, quite close to her.

She puts the ring on her dressing table.

PELLARIN

Sugar . . .

DIANA

Are you going to try to tell me it's a present for *me?*—To make up for the emeralds?

He lowers his eyes. This is a lie he cannot tell.

PELLARIN

I . . . I just found out today—

DIANA

What?

PELLARIN

About the emeralds.

She looks at him . . . Then, with great concentration and practiced skill she sets about the work of repairing her ravaged face. Only the frenetic speed of it betrays her feelings.

PELLARIN (continued)

About your selling off the real ones just to help that first campaign. Why didn't you ever tell me?

DIANA

Why should I?

PELLARIN

I could have tried to thank you.

Silence . . . He feels a terrible compassion for this arid, lonely woman.

PELLARIN (continued)

I'd like another chance to thank you now.

DIANA

Put on your pants. The good ones on the bed. And that's the tie you're wearing. We're meeting La Brandini in the bar.

She continues with her make-up.

DIANA (continued)

I didn't tell you because it was too good a story — You would have made a speech about it for the benefit of every redneck and his wife and hound dog. You would have spread it out all over Washington. What kind of fool would I have looked in just a string of fakes? Isn't it my duty to make everything look real?
  (she rises)
Oh, and don't forget your ring.

She picks up her handbag. Pellarin helps her on with her fur wrap.

PELLARIN

It's pretty warm . . .

DIANA

Not for sable. No way of faking that.

At the door she stops.

DIANA (continued)

Funny . . . you once bought a ring exactly like that — *exactly* like it — for somebody else.

He fails to conceal a startled reaction. She catches him at it.

DIANA (continued)

In Bulgari's some years ago, before the old man died, he showed me the twin of it — thinking I'd be pleased. He'd only made two of them, he told me, and the other had the better

92

ruby: the one he'd sold to you. You'd been through Rome in a great hurry, and he assumed it was for me. But I knew even then who would be getting it . . . She was the one in France.

PELLARIN
(*a low mumble*)
I didn't . . . *take* her there.

DIANA
. . . Alright, you *joined* her there, or found her there, or picked her up . . . and lived there with her like some kind of hippy . . .

She pauses, a gloved hand on the door handle.

DIANA (continued)
Just one thing puzzles me — About the ring . . . Why do you have it now? . . . Is that woman dead?

She waits for an answer . . . doesn't get it, and moves out the door . . . Blake follows her.

DISSOLVE:

63.   INTERIOR. A BEDROOM IN A THIRD-CLASS HOTEL — NIGHT

A gloomy tableau: Stan Loeb, supine on a sagging bed, his hands over his eyes; Dinty Benart in a costive position: slouched forward on a chair, and Sheldon Buckle: erect as a Prussian cadet on review day, staring out the window into the night.

BUCKLE
If I understand you, then, the mission is aborted.

KINZEL
(*coming out of the toilet*)
You poor, miserable klutz — Who said there *was* a "mission" — ?

BUCKLE
I didn't come to you, gentlemen: you sought me out —

LOEB
To do a little seeking, Buckle — not to seek out and destroy.

BUCKLE
(*a bit huffily*)
That was only a suggestion.

Kinzel turns despairingly to the others.

KINZEL
I should have known better, but I didn't want to get the
Company involved —
(*looking suspiciously around*)
Although probably it already *is* . . . Anyway, this was the
only free-lancer in shouting distance.

BUCKLE
The evidence of my discretion is there, gentlemen — on that
table.

Dinty bows his head still lower, and Loeb groans. Strickland comes
out of the bathroom as Kinzel goes to the indicated table, picks up
the little tape recorder and switches it on.

MENAKER'S VOICE: . . . Russia and America squatting on
an "overkill capacity," each weaving scenarios, and filling
"gaps." A scene from Bedlam, Miss Brandini —

BRANDINI'S VOICE: Oh, I *agree* —

MENAKER'S VOICE: (*cutting her off*) In America investment in research and development is the lowest of any country in the world. What are we buying with our cost-plus
contracts? Military spending isn't *investment* — it's
consumption —

Kinzel switches it off.

BUCKLE
It's your man's voice, no doubt of that. He's with some
foreign woman. She's a communist, as well.

STRICKLAND
As well as who?

Loeb is out of bed by now.

LOEB
The immediate problem, Mr. Buckle, is how the fuck you
got your hands on that.

94

BUCKLE
(*a bit subdued*)
She left it in her room.

DINTY
That's all we need—Another break-in!

CUT TO:

64. EXTERIOR. A GARDEN RESTAURANT (LIKE THE RITZ)—
NIGHT

Candles glowing in their glass chimneys on the tables, tiny fairy light
sparkling in the tall trees. Discreet music . . .

Diana—several drinks ahead of her husband and her guest—is
holding forth:

DIANA
Ted—that was the *real* catastrophe . . .

There's no hint of flirtation in it, but Pellarin and Cela Brandini,
pretending to listen, are keenly aware of each other . . . Diana picks
up a brandy bottle and pours out nearly half of it into a nearly empty
pitcher of wine punch.

DIANA (continued)
They call these things *sangrias* . . .

CELA BRANDINI
What interests me is the Vietnam business.

DIANA
(*after a tiny silence*)
There's always too much dago red; the secret is to kill the
taste of orange peel.

PELLARIN
(*to Cela*)
Well, I did *begin*, y'see, as one of Lyndon's boys.

DIANA
So naturally the Goddamn liberals despised him as a Goddamn hawk.

95

CELA BRANDINI
(*turning to Pellarin*)
I thought you broke with Johnson over that?

PELLARIN
A junior congressman doesn't do any "breaking" with a President. I just ran away. The Yippies tried to claim me, but I was too quick for 'em. I joined the Army.

DIANA
The Air Force, dear.

PELLARIN
Thanks for reminding me.

DIANA
(*to Brandini*)
Gene had the universities staked out already, and Bobby was still hoping we'd forget that *his* old boss was *Joe* McCarthy —

PELLARIN
So I escaped the war by going to it.

DIANA
(*quickly to Cela*)
That's a joke, y'understand? Off the record . . . so is everything.

Cela, lighting another cigarette, looks again to Pellarin. He doesn't speak.

DIANA
(*pouring herself another
tall glass of sangria*)
Nobody wanted any heroes from that mess. They were suddenly all Goddamn storm troopers. So Blake was nowhere.

CELA BRANDINI
I thought he was in Paris.

This creates a short, tense silence. Cela has taken them out over some very thin ice.

96

DIANA

*(masking her real feelings with a nervous
little bark of laughter.)*

There was that *phase* . . . For a few months after he got
out of uniform, the Senator resigned from the whole human
race. But that was certainly contem — sorry — temporary.

CELA BRANDINI

I've heard the story . . .

DIANA

Who the hell hasn't? "A period of self-adjustment" — That's
what we all *said* it was.

Pellarin makes no comment. His wife finishes a deep swig of her drink
before she continues:

DIANA

Or premature male menopause.

PELLARIN

(smiling faintly)

That's just a joke, you understand.

DIANA

We hushed it up, and that was one of my mistakes. The
voters have to know he plays around. But they thought for
once he was in love for real, they might have loved him for
it . . .

And loved *me* for forgiving him.

CELA BRANDINI

Have you?

Diana's eyes have lost a little of their normal focus. She's beginning
to suspect that she's allowed herself not only too much drink, but
too much candor.

DIANA

Have I what?

PELLARIN

Forgiven me.

97

DIANA

Sweetie-pie, I never stop.

Her glass is empty. (What the hell — she thinks) and reaches for the big glass pitcher. It's empty, too.

PELLARIN
(*at his most Texan, his eyes
fixed on his wife*)
That would be just peachy-keen, if only there was something *you* were running for.

CELA BRANDINI

I think that Mrs. Pellarin is always running for the same thing.

Diana manages to meet her eyes.

DIANA

Mizz Brandini, that is perfectly correct. I'm running for Blake Pellarin as President of the United States of America.

Cela studies her in silence. Then turns to Pellarin.

CELA BRANDINI

The girl in Paris — the Vietnamese —

DIANA
(*breaking in after a moment*)
She was a half-breed: — Cambodian and French.

CELA BRANDINI
(*to Pellarin*)
Whatever happened to her?

Diana laughs, a short harsh barking sound, quite close to a hiccup.

DIANA

Whatever happened to the monkey?

Silence . . . then:

CUT TO:

65. INTERIOR. A GOOD CHEAP RESTAURANT IN THE OLD
    QUARTER OF MADRID—NIGHT

Kim Menaker looks up from his dinner as Pellarin comes quickly
through the door and sits down opposite him on one of the rickety
little chairs. (His friend is occupying the only comfortable one in
the establishment.)

                    PELLARIN
                    (*as he sits*)
Is it still on—?

                    MENAKER
This time you're *very* late . . .

Boysie, all these great, infernal wads of money—I'm
positively stuffed with it.

                    PELLARIN
You're stuffed with food, for God's sake—What *is* that stuff?

He stares in fascination at the other's plate.

                    MENAKER
Want some?

                    PELLARIN
Thanks. I've already eaten.

                    MENAKER
With your wife, I assume?

                    PELLARIN
No way to get out of it, I'm sorry—

                    MENAKER
And that indecent fortune in your briefcase?

He darts a disapproving glance as Pellarin places it carefully under
the table.

                    MENAKER (continued)
You had time to go to your hotel and put it in the safe. But
I had that appointment—And—

99

PELLARIN

With the brother —

MENAKER

And I was anxious not to keep you waiting for our dinner.

PELLARIN

Some of Diana's snoops were covering the hotel lobby. They could have got to the cashier. That was a can of beans I didn't want to have to open.

MENAKER

I'm carrying a lot of beans. And you've got more.

PELLARIN
(*after a moment*)

You still haven't answered my question.

MENAKER

Is it on? Of course it's on.

PELLARIN
(*relaxing just a little*)

How did you manage it? How did you keep in touch with her through all these years?

MENAKER

The Paris Trib!

PELLARIN

The Paris Herald Tribune?

MENAKER

A phone number. The same date every month: she'd run it in the classified ads. And from all sorts of places: London, Milan, Dusseldorf . . . I was to call the latest number, if it ever happened that I got the chance . . .

PELLARIN

What chance?

MENAKER

To see you, Boysie.

PELLARIN

She had my letter, and she never answered it.

MENAKER

You had my letter and you never answered it.

PELLARIN
(after a silence)
This is between you and me —

MENAKER

Yes, Boysie?

PELLARIN

What *are* those things you're eating?

MENAKER

Eels . . .

PELLARIN
(almost reverently)
Jesus, Kim — I hope so.

MENAKER

Before I lead you to your rendezvous, what do you propose to do with all this money?

PELLARIN
(vaguely)
Buy her a present . . .

MENAKER

Buy who a present?

PELLARIN

Diana, naturally . . .

Menaker's glance betrays a certain malice.

MENAKER

Spicing up your evening with a touch of guilt? Quite useful as an aphrodisiac.

PELLARIN

Kim—Answer me one question.

MENAKER

You're not supposed to ask . . . Your mystery lady was quite firm about it: no questions . . .

PELLARIN

It's just about those . . . eels—

MENAKER

They're tiny *infant* eels.

PELLARIN

They look like worms, that's what they look like.

MENAKER

Practically newborn. The lightest touch of metal utterly destroys them. They're eaten, as you see, with wooden forks . . .

PELLARIN

You've got one in your beard.

Menaker hurriedly rubs at his chin with the tip of the napkin tucked under his collar.

PELLARIN

It got away from you.

Embarrassment disarms the older man, and he decides to smile.

MENAKER

Well, Boysie, that's one distinction they have yet to strip me of. It isn't everyone who nurses lampreys in his whiskers. Shall we introduce another little eel to it and have them multiply? . . . I'll end up like Medusa, and turn my enemies to stone.

PELLARIN

Excuse me—

He fishes delicately for the tiny creature, catches it and brings it forth.

The old man's look is nakedly affectionate.

102

MENAKER

Nobody stays cross with you . . . It's just that this is our
last time together. And it wasn't easy to arrange. The situation with my crazed Field Marshal was rather delicate. By
the way, your helicopter saved my life.

PELLARIN

I didn't send a helicopter —

MENAKER
(*disappointed*)

No?

PELLARIN

How could I? I'm an also-ran. I don't have stuff like that
at my disposal.

MENAKER

They can be chartered privately . . . That didn't occur to
you. It was Brandini, then . . .

PELLARIN
(*breaking in*)

What time *is* it? When am I due — ?

MENAKER

We'll make it comfortably.

He stands up, reaching in his pocket. Blake has already thrown som
money on the table — clearly a good deal more than necessary. Th
two move out together —

66. EXTERIOR. THE STREET IN FRONT OF THE RESTAURANT -
NIGHT

They are looking for a cab when a waiter rushes up to them.

WAITER

Señor — !

PELLARIN

Yes?

WAITER
(*handing it to him*)

You forgot your briefcase.

103

Pellarin tips him, and during this, Menaker, who has brought himself a brandy bottle from the restaurant, takes a swig.

                    MENAKER
Easy for you . . .

                    PELLARIN
You take it easy with that booze —

                    MENAKER
               (*starting down the street*)
You've got 'em neat and tidy in your little Wall Street case.
But I can feel pesetas leaking out of me like straw from an
old scarecrow.

67. TRAVELING SHOT (LOUMAR)

                    PELLARIN
You're half stoned already.

                    MENAKER
I'm no such thing. I'm twice as drunk as you are.

                    PELLARIN
What's that got to do with it?

                    MENAKER
And I'm twice as old. That also is irrelevant . . . And not
quite true.

But Pellarin is paying no attention. His thoughts are in another country. He's bad-tempered, full of anxiety and raging doubts.

                    PELLARIN
I took her out of Phnom Penh, and we went to Paris . . .
Then, suddenly, she left me — Why? . . .

                    MENAKER
The money isn't mine, you know. It isn't yours. It's
nobody's . . .

                    PELLARIN
Keep it — !

104

MENAKER
(*with something like a leer*)
You're trying to get rid of everything, aren't you? — Mostly other people's property.

PELLARIN
She had my letter. You gave it to her, Kim.

MENAKER
Wasn't there money in that envelope?

PELLARIN
Dear Christ, there's too much money in this whole affair . . . Money, emeralds, a ruby ring . . .

The ring is in his hand. He looks down at it.

PELLARIN (continued)
She really threw it at you?

MENAKER
Oh, yes.

PELLARIN
Perhaps the money was what did it. Could she have thought that I was paying her off . . . as though she was some streetwalker — ?

MENAKER
She may still be wondering. That could be the purpose of this operation . . .

PELLARIN
(*suddenly*)
It was a *horse*, Goddamnit!

MENAKER
(*after a startled moment*)
Did you say *horse* — ?

PELLARIN
The one she fancied: "Cavalier" . . . Near where we lived there was a bartender who used to take our bets, and she was crazy for the races. So when you came and yanked me

off to Switzerland, I put something down for her on Cavalier. It paid terrific odds. I knew she didn't read the papers, so I thought that I'd surprise her, and put her winnings with my letter—The one I gave to you . . .

Silence . . .

I explained it all. About the money—Everything. How soon I'd be coming back. And how I'd never leave her, even for a day, until I died . . .

Silence . . .

Then she . . . she disappeared . . . *Why*—? . . . And why has she come back?

For some time Menaker has disappeared into the shadows. Now a quiet tinkling is heard.

MENAKER'S VOICE
All I know, old darling, is what I read in the papers.

PELLARIN
I hate you when you're being cute.

MENAKER'S VOICE
You find it . . . unbecoming?
(*he starts to recite*)
"You are old, Father William," the young man said, "And yet you persistently stand on your head, Do you think at your age it is right?"

He emerges, in the words of London's urinals: "adjusting his dress."

PELLARIN
Yes, I find it unbecoming—*And* unbelievable—

MENAKER
Here's a taxi.

He waves it to a halt and they get in.

68.   INTERIOR. TAXI—NIGHT

MENAKER
(*after a moment*)
Unbelievable?

106

PELLARIN

Paris is what really bothers me.

MENAKER

Paris?

PELLARIN

The whole Goddamn *coincidence*.

Menaker looks blank, but it's possible to suspect that he is not as drunk as he would like to seem (or maybe like to be).

The cab continues through the narrow streets (Menaker having issued some instructions when they entered it).

PELLARIN

You, Kim, just *happened* to be passing by — through Paris, for God's sake!

MENAKER

You'd been out of circulation much too long. I came to get you to that conference. There were photographs with Maxwell Taylor and McCloy. That was important for you.

PELLARIN

Geneva . . . that was where I finally made my mind up —

MENAKER

Besides old Amos Streeter had just died —

PELLARIN
(*cutting him off*)

There's the coincidence!

MENAKER
(*after a short, exasperated silence*)

On the other side of the Atlantic an antique statesman expires from a surfeit of Kentucky bourbon on his senatorial toilet seat — that's your coincidence?

PELLARIN

Well, it's why you came. It's why you managed — Christ knows how — to break it up between me and the only girl I ever loved.

107

MENAKER

Now how could I do that?

PELLARIN

All I know is *why* . . . Streeter was gone and now you
thought my chance had finally come and you could run me
for the senate —

(*he breaks off . . . Then, sharply*)

Diana sent you, didn't she?

MENAKER

I paid my own fare, Boysie.

PELLARIN

Well you got what you were after — you got me back to
Washington —

MENAKER

The woman left you.

The words ring in Pellarin's ears . . .

PELLARIN

You left the conference. You went back two days ahead of
me. What did you say to her?

A heavy silence filled with tension.

MENAKER

There was that lovely park along the Seine . . . They've
made a highway out of it, a parking lot . . . or something.
That hadn't happened yet.

We took a little stroll down there. This being, as no doubt
you'll remember, Paris in the spring.

Silence.

MENAKER (continued)

She seemed to understand how short a time that season lasts
. . . The observation came from her.

PELLARIN

What came from *you*?

108

MENAKER
(*after a moment*)
I told her you were born for greatness . . . That your whole
life had been a preparation for it.

PELLARIN
And that impressed her?

MENAKER
No, not very much.

PELLARIN
I shouldn't think so. I was through with politics. I knew it
in Geneva, and I wrote her that. You took the letter to her.
I said that I was coming back to marry her.

MENAKER
Get a divorce and marry her — Yes, that *was* the plan . . .

PELLARIN
People do it all the time.

MENAKER
And where would you be now?

PELLARIN
Still in the rue Jacob, maybe. I might still be happy.

The old man's face is flushed with sudden anger.

MENAKER
You're a political animal — not Rudolfo in La Vie Boheme!

He speaks with an abrupt and sober ferocity:

I'll tell you what I *didn't* tell her — I didn't say that if our
candidate should ever drop that lovely lady, his good
wife — to marry what would be described in Texas as a half-
breed Asiatic —

He breaks off — partly silenced by the look in Blake's eye, and also
by the noise: canned music, loud and various, blaring out . . . There's
a great yelping of barkers, the clatter of shooting galleries, the click-
ety rattle of the wheels of fortune . . . The cab has moved into the
glare of many lights.

109

MENAKER
(*shouting an explanation*)
The Verbena de San Juan—

PELLARIN
What?

MENAKER
A kind of feria—

PELLARIN
You mean she's *here*—?

MENAKER
How do I know?

The cab turns a corner where a large, dark house blots out much
of the lights, and baffles much of the sound. Menaker gives money
to the driver, and gets out, Pellarin following. The taxi coughs, and
rattles off into the night.

69.   EXTERIOR. STREET (FRESH ANGLE)—NIGHT

PELLARIN
(*after a pause*)
Kim . . .

MENAKER
Yes?

PELLARIN
Is this whole Goddamn thing another trick of yours?

It's a cool night, but the sweat is pouring down Kim Menaker's face.

MENAKER
Our coming to Madrid? Oh, yes, it was a kind of trick . . .
This much is true: she wants to see you . . .
(*slight pause*)
Don't ask me why . . . That might be just another trick.

The tall, old building, all its shutters firmly closed, looms darkly
over them across the street.

The carnival sounds: the muted growl and clatter of the Verbena
Fair and weirdly echoed from the other side of the dark house.

MENAKER

Hold on there —

Pellarin has started moving toward the house. He stops.

MENAKER (continued)

This is *her* story . . . You enter it only when she says you
enter.

PELLARIN

And when is that?

MENAKER

(*with a sudden hint of mischief*)

"When the bawdy hand of the dial is on the prick" of midnight . . . Then I suppose you turn into a pumpkin.

Pellarin stands waiting in the street.

What is it you expect? . . .

Silence.

Her story is your dream . . . But what is it you've been
dreaming?

Does Blake attempt (and fail) to find an answer? . . . He is in deep
shadow and Kim can only guess.

MENAKER (continued)

I was the one who picked the town; and luckily, it seems
she owns a house here, too . . . That sounds, doesn't it, as
if your lady's rich — ?

PELLARIN

Rich . . . ?

MENAKER

There are so many possibilities. Primo: she is very, *very* rich:
the mistress, maybe, of a ship owner in Greece . . .

PELLARIN

Your eyes are going back on you.

MENAKER

Why? What's there to see?

111

PELLARIN

That sign. It says that house is up for sale.

MENAKER

She could be moving to the country . . . to another country . . . For all I know, old darling—

Pellarin cuts him off.

PELLARIN

I wish you wouldn't call me that.

MENAKER

The expression is quite innocent, Senator. I was just going
to say that she might well be poor.

A brief silence . . . Then Menaker continues. (Is there a whiff of
malice in his tone? We can't be sure.)

MENAKER

Or shall we say just *medium* poor? A vendeuse on the rue
de Rivoli—you know, those dinky little shops that sell fake
perfume to the tourists. An usherette in some cheap, stink-
ing cinema . . . She could be *very* poor. She could be
hungry. More women than you'd ever guess are hungry . . .
And finally—well, you told me once she had connections
with her King.

PELLARIN

The Cambodians.

MENAKER

And that she styles herself "Princess"?

PELLARIN

Oh, yes. She's that. A royal princess.

MENAKER

Dear boy, you've got to be prepared for anything

He waits a moment; then goes on:

There are bordellos full of royalty.

Pellarin turns into the light. His face is white with rage.

112

PELLARIN

You're telling me that she's a prostitute?

Silence . . .

MENAKER

Whatever she is, Boysie, it's her secret . . . Suppose, just
for the sake of argument, she *is* hungry and she has to walk
the streets. Does it matter to you what she's *doing*—or what
she *is*?

PELLARIN
*(after a moment, staring
up at the house)*

She must want me to know—

MENAKER

Perhaps she wants to show you what you missed—To see
if you can still be hurt—To show you that she's grown more
beautiful—Women are both vain and cruel—

Pellarin cuts him off, sharply.

PELLARIN

Since when are *you* an authority on women?

This was a bit below the belt, and Kim can't manage a reply.

PELLARIN

Anyway, why shouldn't she be cruel?

MENAKER
(heaving a sigh)

You poor self-pitying booby! They won't let you walk into
a room two years from now without a brass band playing
"Hail to the Chief."

PELLARIN

What's that to her?

A pause.

MENAKER

She may want to ruin it.

Blake stares at him.

113

MENAKER (continued)
She may want you back.

70.   FRESH ANGLE

Blake turns away a little . . . the noises of the feria are muted now, melting together, like the murmur of some crazy ocean.

PELLARIN

She had a way of walking—a special way . . . a kind of striding rhythm that her heels made on the pavement. I'd recognize it anywhere.

Three years ago I was in Paris . . . I was in Paris every time I could invent some kind of an excuse . . . I was still searching for some trace of her.

Where the Boulevard Sainte Michel opens out onto the quai: that's where it happened. About this time of night, about this time of year—I was standing there when suddenly—I heard those footsteps. And it seemed to me (just for a moment) that my girl was moving toward me—hurrying forward—as though she'd found me in that crowd . . .

I stood there waiting for her touch: the way she used to take me by the sleeve.

I didn't turn . . . I was afraid to turn . . . I knew that there was no one there.

In some distant bell tower, the hour begins to toll.

Blake Pellarin faces the old house. As he moves toward it, a heavy shadow swallows him . . .

An urgent whistling sound: then the bright boom and crackle of some fireworks.

In the brief glare, Kim Menaker can see the door just closing . . .

CUT TO:

71.   INTERIOR. THE OLD, DARK HOUSE

Once the home of some prosperous merchant in another century. Such remnants of a discreet luxury as still remain can only give out dusty hints of what had been their mild pomposity. The rest are ghosts, shrouded in sheets.

114

The scene is strange, almost surreal . . . (The action must be given in synopsis . . . The climax of this sequence is strongly erotic: to spell out its specific details would be to risk pornography) . . .

A man searching and searching — up and down, from floor to floor, from room to room of an empty house, comes to discover (in a lightning flash of fireworks breaking through a shuttered window) that all along there has been someone watching him: — naked, in a shadowed chair.

This enigmatic presence, for long years, has occupied his every dream . . .

He kneels before her . . . Places the ring back on her finger . . . Then speaks to her — at first, in a few whispered monosyllables . . .

Her replies come slowly, teasingly . . . Delphic in the meaning he must choose from . . .

All this is in French . . . English subtitles, without the visual element, are inescapably banal.

What is essential is not what happens, but the way it is shown: the echoing vacancy of the big house . . . the jeering racket of the carnival . . . the blast of fireworks beyond the blinds . . .

. . . Why?

— *why*?!

Why did she leave him? He'd promised, back in Paris, to return to her in just two days. He'd stayed away less than a day longer — but he'd *explained* — he'd written everything . . .

Why was it that she'd run away?

And why are they here now, together, after all these empty years?

There is no end to all his questions.

But in her arms she puts the last of them to silence . . .

CUT TO:

72. EXTERIOR. THE STREET OUTSIDE — NIGHT

Kim Menaker, weary of just standing there, and staring at the blind old house, wanders off into the little feria . . . among the wheels of fortune, shooting galleries and the carousel . . .

He finds himself, after an idle time, riding the ferris wheel.

115

73. INTERCUT

As Menaker rides round and round . . . catching a fleeting glimpse, each time around, of the open window in the room where the two inside the house go on and on with love-making . . .

74. FRESH ANGLE

Often there must be a stop to change the passengers. And once this brings him opposite that open window.

75. REVERSE ANGLE

Pellarin, naked, stands there.

Kim is just across from him, like a great child rocking in its cradle.

76. INTERCUT

They watch each other . . .

Neither can move . . .

Then, with a jerk and fresh spurt of music, the ferris wheel starts turning, and Kim is taken from the scene . . .

DISSOLVE:

77. INTERIOR. THE HOUSE

An air of celebration:

(SUBTITLE) Blake says that what is needed is some wine.

He starts down the stairs (SUBTITLE) Where, he asks, is the wine cellar?

A mocking voice calls down to him:

>   VOICE
>   (*in excellent English*)
>   You might look in the cellar . . .

Blake, calling back, asks where she's learned her English?

But she doesn't answer.

Continuing down to the cellar he shouts louder, asking for her preference in wine. Then, laughing, answers himself:

PELLARIN
Why do I ask? With us, wasn't it always Burgundy —

78. INTERIOR. WINE CELLAR

He finds a reasonable choice, picks a bottle which he thinks will please her, and bounds back up the stairs again —

79. INTERIOR. WHAT HAS BECOME "THEIR BEDROOM"

It's empty.

Her clothes have vanished —

She has gone.

CUT TO:

80. INTERIOR. A SMALL CAFE

From a window table there's a view of the old house.

Here Kim Menaker sits and drinks his brandy.

And waits . . .

CUT BACK TO:

81. INTERIOR. THE HOUSE

And now Blake Pellarin has recommenced a search which had begun nine years ago:

From floor to floor . . . from one empty room after another . . .

Tonight — all through their happy time together — he had kept on pelting her with the same question: —

Why — ? . . . Why . . . ?

Now the question is repeated . . .

(He feels that he'll go on repeating it until the day he dies.)

DISSOLVE:

82. INTERIOR. THE CAFE

Some instinct brings Kim Menaker to his feet . . . He moves out into —

83. EXTERIOR. THE STREET BEFORE THE HOUSE – NIGHT

Menaker stands waiting . . .

Pause.

The door opens.

Menaker starts forward –

Pellarin passes him without a word . . .

84. TRAVELING SHOT – NIGHT

Blake Pellarin keeps on walking . . .

Kim realizes that Blake is caught up in an experience he cannot share . . . But he follows . . . At first, trying to catch up with him . . . Then, simply dogging along behind . . .

Pellarin stops.

Menaker stops.

Pellarin turns and looks back at him.

The look is blank – so totally dismissive that Kim gives up: He cannot speak or move.

He stands there, watching his friend go . . .

The fireworks have come to their finale: a sustained quivering flare of light reveals the emptiness of the long, narrow street. The popping scatter of the little colored bombs seem to him, for a moment, to be accompanied by the chant of the little children:

"Quiene tiene miedo . . ."

The colored lights fall into darkness . . .

Kim Menaker turns back into –

85. INTERIOR. THE SMALL CAFE

He gets another drink from the sleepy barman, and takes it back to his old table by the window . . . Two pimps finish their card game, and Kim raises his head to watch them go.

86. REVERSE ANGLE

He sees instead – Blake Pellarin looking at him on the far side of the glass.

Kim's face (reflected in the window) lights up with joy —

87.   FRESH ANGLE

He rises as the door opens and Blake enters.

An icy chill of realization grips Kim's heart as he sees that his friend
has not come back here to make peace.

> PELLARIN
> (*dropping some change on the bar top*)
> I want to call a cab.

The command is given in his bad Spanish . . . He turns and faces
Kim.

> PELLARIN (continued)
> You didn't give it to her.

Kim doesn't answer.

> You never meant for her to have it . . . You stole my letter.

> MENAKER
> Yes, Boysie.

Blake moves up to him.

> If you're going to strike me, do it now and get it over with.

> PELLARIN
> If I laid a hand on you, I'd murder you.

Kim struggles, and brings up a small attempt at an ironic joke.

> MENAKER
> You can't afford it, Boysie. It's a long way from here to Penn-
> sylvania Avenue.

> PELLARIN
> Screw Pennsylvania Avenue.

> MENAKER
> Boysie — There's nowhere else for you to go.

But then he wilts under the look Blake gives him.

119

88. EXTERIOR. THE STREET OUTSIDE THE CAFE—NIGHT

Pellarin comes out of the cafe. After an anguished moment, Kim Menaker catches up with him . . .

They stand together waiting for the taxi . . .

> MENAKER
> (*after a moment*)
> I didn't see her go . . . There must be other doors—

Silence.

> PELLARIN
> About that letter—she told me she had never seen it. Just the money in the envelope . . .
>
> What I'd written was that I would never leave her, even for a day, until I died. I made her the same promises again tonight . . . and all she did was laugh . . .
>
> And I laughed with her, hoping to put myself into her mind . . . That's something you can never do.

> MENAKER
> I didn't see her leave the house. There must be other doors . . .

A night taxi comes rattling down the street and halts. Pellarin calls out to the driver asking him to wait. Then, from the envelope he takes a roll of old French francs.

> PELLARIN
> I never guessed the truth until I found the envelope—
> (*he looks down at it*)
> I searched for her in every room and this is what I found . . . the same amount of money that I'd left her . . . on a dressing table all those years ago . . . . I thought it was a note from *her*. But no, it was my envelope. The same I'd given you eight years ago to bring her from Geneva—

He holds up a wad of old francs under Kim's nose.

> You're a gentleman, I keep forgetting that. You don't read other people's mail—you tear it up!

The look in Menaker's face is his reply.

PELLARIN (continued)
You didn't even talk to her. You merely left the money in
the envelope and put it on her dressing table—Like you'd
pay a whore—!

With a sudden movement, he stuffs the money into a side pocket
of Kim's jacket.

Give it back to her—

He moves to the waiting cab.

MENAKER
I can't . . . I can't . . . I don't know where to find her.

Blake stops by the cab door.

PELLARIN
I think the two of you were after the same thing. Deep in
your bones you wanted me to hurt . . . To feel something—
if it was only pain.

He gets into the car . . . Kim moves to the window.

MENAKER
Then . . . this is the real thing?

PELLARIN
The real what?

MENAKER
The real good-bye.

PELLARIN
It isn't paste, "old darling." It's just shit . . . For Christ's sake,
stop that blubbering.

MENAKER
Who's blubbering? . . . I've got a whole lot of your money.
Who shall I give it to?

PELLARIN
There's got to be another boy out there—on some park
bench . . .

He yanks a handkerchief from his pocket, and, without looking,
tosses it through the window. It hits Kim Menaker in the face.

121

The taxi drives away.

Kim stands watching it go . . . catching his breath.

And then starts walking up the street . . .

89. REVERSE ANGLE

Blake's briefcase stands forgotten on the street in front of the cafe.

90. NEW SCENE

Turning into a wider street, Kim comes to a sudden halt. He hears
the sound of a car—Can it be Blake returning? . . . Kim hurries
back . . .

91. THE STREET CORNER (NEAR THE CAFE)—NIGHT

The taxi stops. Blake gets out and pays the driver. He moves toward
the briefcase just as Kim comes panting to the opposite street corner.

Across this distance, their eyes meet.

PELLARIN

You want the taxi?

MENAKER

No.

PELLARIN

Then tell him not to wait.

Kim Menaker calls out to the driver, and the cab clatters away into
the darkness.

After a moment, Pellarin starts across the street toward Menaker
who waits for him expectantly.

Pellarin approaches . . .

And passes him without a word . . .

MENAKER
(calling after him)

You should have kept the taxi . . . I mean, with all that
money . . .

Pellarin has all but vanished in the shadows.

92. REVERSE ANGLE (LOUMAR)—NIGHT

Menaker tries to catch up with him, but with the best speed he can manage, Pellarin remains somewhere ahead, invisible . . . Yet Menaker can hear his quickening footsteps . . .

He stops to listen . . . to make sure of the direction the sound is coming from . . . He feels totally disoriented, and stands there weaving like a drunkard . . .

He staggers and almost falls onto a window ledge . . . He sits there gasping for breath . . .

A plane passes overhead.

> "Quien tiene Miedo del tri-mo-tor . . .
> del tri-mo-tor . . ."

In a half whisper he has been repeating the children's little chant. Then suddenly he stops—

For just a moment he'd imagined he could hear the echo of those voices drifting like a tiny, chill wind over the dreaming city . . .

He rises, and stands listening—

Silence.

FADE OUT (1/4 DISSOLVE)

FADE IN:

93. ENTRANCE OF THE HOTEL PALACE—NIGHT

Blake arrives, climbs the steps to the door, but doesn't enter.

94. HIS VIEWPOINT

Through the glass he can make out some members of his staff sprawled out unattractively in the hotel lobby. They'll wake if he comes in, and he can't bear to face them . . .

95. EXTERIOR. HOTEL—NIGHT

He turns away; but something stops him before he can start down the stairs—a dark figure lurking ominously in the shadows.

                    PELLARIN
          (*the politician's automatic response*)
     Hi, there.

123

(he squints into the darkness)
You're . . . ah . . .

BUCKLE
(taking a short step into the light)
We've never met, Senator. And I suggest you would be well-advised to keep it that way.

In his professional career, Pellarin has grown accustomed to almost every sort of confrontation. This one, he decides, is just another kook.

BUCKLE
I have a message.

(slight pause)
It's for your . . . "friend."

The portentous manner in which this statement is delivered has made Blake aware of just how tired he really is.

PELLARIN
Which friend is that?

BUCKLE
Why, Menaker, of course.

PELLARIN
I won't be seeing Doctor Menaker.

He moves down toward the street where he is caught in the sudden glare of headlights . . . Cela Brandini has turned them on. At the wheel of her jeep she looks dauntingly professional, as though she were about to cross the Gobi desert.

CELA BRANDINI
You're up late, Pellarin.

PELLARIN
You're up early.

CELA BRANDINI
I guess we both have an early flight . . . Get in.

PELLARIN
Don't tell anybody, but I kind of think I'll take the train.

124

CELA BRANDINI
Don't you have a speech to make in Brussels?

He looks at her a trifle blankly; then moves around to the passenger's side of the jeep.

96. FRESH ANGLE

On the way he is again accosted by J. Sheldon Buckle.

BUCKLE
(*in an undertone, as though passing on an important secret*)
If you *do* see him — you might just tell him that he's lucky.

PELLARIN
Menaker? — *Lucky*?

BUCKLE
My mission from the outset was unclear, and now it's been aborted. He can set his mind at rest.

Silent as a stalking Indian, Buckle moves back into the shadows.

CELA BRANDINI
(*as Pellarin sits down beside her*)
Who the hell was that?

DINTY
Senator —

97. FRESH ANGLE

Dinty Benart hurrying down the steps.

PELLARIN
Dinty —

DINTY
Yes, Senator?

PELLARIN
Who's the goof-ball?

125

DINTY

That's what he is, Senator. The man's bananas. Somebody
tried to loan him to us, but don't worry: I'll kick Buckle's
ass back where he came from—

CELA BRANDINI

Back where, exactly?

DINTY

Who knows? Back to some jungle, maybe, to shoot a few
more jigaboos—
                    (quick change of tone)
Driving the boss out to the airport, Mizz Brandini?

CELA BRANDINI

Wherever he decides to go—

The motor's running; she steps on the gas . . . Dinty—worried as
usual—watches them go.

98.   EXTERIOR. THE JEEP—NIGHT

They roar up the street, past the Cortes, and on into the Gran Via
(its nineteenth-century eccentricities showing their silhouettes against
the pallid sky) . . .

CELA BRANDINI

Tell me what you'll say in Brussels.

The last thing on earth that Blake wants to talk about is Brussels.
But he's a politician.

PELLARIN

Oh . . . I guess I'll use my little gag about the button: the
Big Bang button. Vote for president, you're voting for the
man who gets to push it. And we can be damn certain that
he'll do it in the safety and comfort of the presidential bomb
shelter—a mile or so under the earth.

CELA BRANDINI

So what's the "gag"?

PELLARIN

A small addition to the oath of office: if a president so much
as puts a finger on that button, he has to stay up here with
all the rest of us.

126

CELA BRANDINI

That's a little stupid.

PELLARIN

Sure, but it'll play in Brussels. Peace, arms limitation — that's what the meeting's all about. My mission, as an also-ran, is to get noticed.

CELA BRANDINI

Well, if you've still got the Nobel on your mind —

PELLARIN
(cutting in)
A friend of mine says that the button joke should wait for the campaign: the last day or so — like Eisenhower's promise to make that personal visit to Korea. That way he figures they won't have time to find the holes in it.

CELA BRANDINI

Holes? The thing's a sieve. Who *does* go underground?

PELLARIN

Who cares? In the long run, honey — what'll it matter?

CELA BRANDINI

I know that friend . . . I used to think I liked him . . .

PELLARIN
(after a silence)
Turn left at the next corner, then sharp right until you get to a cafe —

98. EXTERIOR. NARROW STREETS

CELA BRANDINI

Who are you looking for — Your friend? I would have thought you'd seen enough of Kimball Menaker.

PELLARIN

I owe him an apology . . .

She sighs with exasperation.

127

CELA BRANDINI

Oh, *you* — !

PELLARIN

You're right, sugar — Oh, me.

CELA BRANDINI

You always seem to be so . . . so *burdened.*

PELLARIN

That's what you're going to write about me?

CELA BRANDINI

If I write about you.

PELLARIN

Which means you're through with me?

CELA BRANDINI

Or vice versa.

Silence, while she drives.

CELA BRANDINI (continued)

There was a time, not very long ago, when we were both
agreed on something.

PELLARIN

And what could that have been?

CELA BRANDINI

I think we wanted to make love.

PELLARIN
(*after a moment*)

There it is — the far side of that little square.

CELA BRANDINI

What happened? . . . Why has it changed for both of us?

PELLARIN
(*retreating into his deepest Texan*)

That's just pure melancholy speculation, Missy. It's just a
big ole barrel a' squirmin' worms . . . Right here is where
we stop.

128

99. EXTERIOR. THE STREET IN FRONT OF THE SMALL CAFE —
NIGHT

They stop a little short of it.

CELA BRANDINI
I saw a lot of worms myself a little while ago. One of your
loyal staff gave me a little treat —

He looks at her for a moment, and then climbs out of the jeep.

PELLARIN
Leave it lay. I'd rather wait and read your version.

CELA BRANDINI
(staring in front of her)
I *did* like him . . .

PELLARIN
Who's this?

CELA BRANDINI
And I don't like myself at all for changing my opinion.

PELLARIN
Kim Menaker? If you'll excuse the expression, he can go fuck
himself.

CELA BRANDINI
That's just what he's been doing.

PELLARIN
Yes . . . he's done a real good job on that.

She is still looking straight ahead, her hands gripping the wheel.

CELA BRANDINI
After all . . . who doesn't masturbate?

He stands quite still, looking at her, his face ghastly under the mer-
cury street lamp.

CELA BRANDINI (continued)
It's that scifoso handkerchief . . .

PELLARIN

Scifoso? . . . that means dirty.

CELA BRANDINI

Scifo*sissimo*. One of your loyal followers filled me in on
it this evening. I'm ashamed for you and that old man—
But mostly, I'm ashamed that I'm so bothered by it.

PELLARIN

Whose handkerchief?

CELA BRANDINI

You don't know about it? — You really don't?

She turns to look at him, incredulous.

PELLARIN

I really don't.

CELA BRANDINI

They must have kept it from you.

PELLARIN

They do a lot of that.

CELA BRANDINI

It was found among those letters . . . During his sexual fan-
tasizing about you—Dr. Menaker would masturbate into
a handkerchief of yours . . . Then, when it was stiff with
his dried semen, he mailed it to his crippled friend, as . . .
I don't know what: a sentimental souvenir.

PELLARIN

A handkerchief . . . !

Pellarin has turned away. He utters a sudden, terrible groan.

She looks at the anguished profile, its outline etched in the street
light's hectic yellow glow.

CELA BRANDINI
(*almost whispering*)

Success—

130

PELLARIN
(*a low murmur*)
I threw one at his face.

CELA BRANDINI
That is your real burden. Not your failures and mistakes,
your personal regrets. Success — that's the heavy stone tied
to your neck.

She waits. He doesn't speak.

She drives off — rather noisily.

He takes a faltering step or two in the direction of the cafe.

At that instant the lights go off. The sleepy proprietor starts pulling
down the shades.

Too late to call back Cela —

Blake starts walking.

He had gone from one room to another, searching for his love, and
knowing she was lost to him . . . Now he wanders through the dark
streets of the city, searching — just as vainly — for his friend . . .

DISSOLVE:

100. SERIES OF SHOTS — NIGHT

Blake Pellarin has come into an unfamiliar place: some ghastly hous-
ing scheme, new in the last days of the Generalissimo, and already
fallen into the sordid decay of cheap construction . . . Buildings like
big ugly boxes are crammed together on the barren earth where not
a tree or blade of grass is growing . . .

Some highway he has never seen before provides — with its
overpass — a kind of city gate to this collection of seemingly deserted
hives and, with stumbling footsteps, he hastens toward its shelter.

Clinging by an arm to one of the concrete arches, he starts to retch:
a cursing, sobbing noise.

It wakes a nearby sleeper . . .

Blake reaches in a pocket for a handkerchief, and brings out instead,
a shower of paper money . . . Then he hears a noise —

131

The noise repeats itself: a sinister rattle, as though some monstrous baby were crouching in the shadows.

He turns, following the sound . . .

He sees a terribly distorted figure seated in a sort of wheelchair. A claw of a hand is shaking something: a tin can with a few coins in it. The face looks like a skull.

Blake, confronted by this terrifying apparition, weaves a bit on his unsteady legs . . . then takes a hesitant step forward . . .

And now he sees that the black, empty sockets are, in fact, a blind man's glasses.

Staggering a little, he bends down, opens the briefcase, and seizes up some of the money. Straightening, he tries to bring himself to move with it to the creature in the wheelchair.

Again — almost derisively — there comes the rattle of the cup.

Pellarin throws the money on the beggar's lap. Much of it flutters to the earth. He grabs more and throws it . . .

Silence . . .

Then, once again, the rattle of the cup.

More and more money — in a kind of frenzy, he flings it at the blind man — faster and faster . . .

These wild gestures are not made in charity, but in terror and black hatred — not of the beggar, but of something in the depths of his own spirit . . .

An instinctive sense of this has reached the cripple: a sense of danger . . . He awaits his chance . . .

Again, bearing a great load of money, Blake bends to drop it in the beggar's lap. The hand strikes out like a rattlesnake.

His wrist is gripped with an astonishing and terrible strength. He strains with all his force to free himself, but can't. The talons of that claw are like the steel teeth of a trap.

In desperation, he gets the white cane, and kicks out at the rickety old chair — a wheel breaks, and the beggar falls, still clinging to his wrist.

The black glasses are knocked off. Two seeing eyes, the color of spit, glare up at him. The claw feels like the hand of death itself dragging him down into the grave.

132

Blinded by fear and loathing, Pellarin strikes out again—

Silence.

The pale gray eyes are truly sightless now. The skull-like face, bloody and shattered, rests in a garbage heap of paper money.

Blake's eyes are on the corpse, but he is looking down a long dark corridor with no glimpse of an exit at the end of it.

FADE OUT (1/4 DISSOLVE).

FADE IN:

101. EXTERIOR. HOTEL PALACE—BRIGHT, VERY EARLY MORNING

Everybody up, all dressed and ready for the plane trip. Especially Diana. She's perfectly controlled and in control of everything.

DIANA
Isn't there a train from here to France?

Her followers look blank. The Hotel's chief Conserje steps forward.

CONSERJE
Madame, there's the Rapido to San Sebastian—

DINTY
How far is that from Brussels?

Strickland groans at this display of ignorance.

CONSERJE
The train goes to the frontier. The French frontier.

STRICKLAND
That takes all day—!

DIANA
He'll think it's perfect. You know how crazy Blake is about trains.
            (with a kind of grim satisfaction)
We'll find him at the railroad station.

133

CONSERJE
(*consulting his watch*)
Too late, I'm afraid. The Rapido leaves at just —

DIANA
(*cutting him off*)
We'll have to phone ahead to the first place it stops — a

CONSERJE
It doesn't stop, Madame.

A brief, awkward silence. Then:

CONSERJE (continued)
Senator will take a plane to Brussels from Bordeaux.

DIANA
How do *you* know?

CONSERJE
He phoned and asked for those arrangements.

DIANA
(*brightly*)
Well, I suppose it's alright if he makes it . . . And after all —
what can happen to him on a train?

CUT TO:

102. INTERIOR. THE RAILROAD STATION — EARLY MORNING

Pellarin, about to board the Rapido, is firmly but politely halted by
an Inspector of Police. He is attended by uniformed policemen and
detectives in plain clothes.

The Inspector is fully aware of the importance of this U.S. Senator.
So he puts the whole thing most discreetly:

There has been an incident . . . In fact, a murder. Some wretched
beggar killed in obscure circumstances . . . It is definitely *not* a matter
for the Senator's concern . . . However, quite close to the scene of
the crime, this was found —

He produces the briefcase.

Considering the amount of money it contains, the Inspector indicates
a certain surprise that the proper authorities had not been notified

134

of its theft. It is his privilege to return it to the Distinguished Senator, and wish him a good trip.

With mumbled thanks, the Distinguished Senator receives (once again) his briefcase, and climbs up into the train.

Signals are made for its departure.

Trailing behind him a lengthening wake of disaster, and bearing with him all his burdens, Blake Pellarin has resumed his shadowed quest . . .

We wait for the expected fade out . . .

The Inspector and his staff wait politely for the train to leave . . .

103. INTERIOR. TRAIN CAR

Pellarin, making his way down the corridor, stops suddenly—

Through the sliding door he has caught sight of a passenger—Kim Menaker.

Their eyes meet in a kind of mutual horror.

Kim speaks at last, and with some difficulty:

                    MENAKER
     I'll get straight off. I *was* booked through to Paris—Oh, God!
     I think the train is starting—

CUT TO:.

104. EXTERIOR. THE STATION PLATFORM

The Inspector of Police has noticed the Distinguished Senator in one of the train windows.

The Senator is waving—

CUT TO:

105. KIM'S COMPARTMENT

Pellarin is leaning out the window . . . We hear his sharp cry—

The police are moving forward . . . toward the train—

CUT TO:

106. THE STATION PLATFORM

It is now observed that what the Senator is actually doing is negotiating the purchase from the vending cart of a large bottle of brandy.

And just in time: the train has started to move . . .

107. SERIES OF SHOTS

Just too late for Cela Brandini who comes racing into the scene (immediately capturing the full attention of the police).

She is dressed as usual: semi-safari with a strong hint of battle fatigues, a costume normally offensive to the more formal Spanish eye. But in the flush of her exasperation at missing the train, the police find her irresistible.

From the open window of the Senator's compartment, Cela can just make out two male voices raised in song: (Kim's hit number from the Hasty Pudding Show of nineteen twenty-nine)

THEIR VOICES
"Oh, it makes me kind of sad,
To think about Sir Galahad—"

Turning from the pretty girl, the Inspector salutes the departing train—

Blake and Kim have six more hours together.

"To amuse a girl and charm her
He would jump into his armor
And joust away until . . .

Cela watches as the train pulls out of the station.

(If you want a happy
ending, that depends,
of course, on where
you stop your story.)

AFTERWORD

He is a great man — like all great men he is never satisfied that he has chosen the right path in life. Even being President, he feels, may somehow not be right. He is a man who has within him the devil of self-destruction that lives in every genius. You know that you're absolutely great, there is no question of that, but have you chosen the right road? Should I be a monk? Should I jerk off in the park? Should I just fuck everybody and forget about everything else? Should I be President? It is not self-doubt; it is cosmic doubt! What am I going to do — I am the best, I know that, now what do I do with it?

Hannibal crossed the Alps with the second greatest army in classical history. He arrived at the outer gates of Rome and Rome was in his hands, ready to be taken. At the outer gates, he stopped and went back. What made him stop? That same devil — this thing that always stops conquerors at the moment of victory. That is what The Big Brass Ring *is about. Also: There is this foolish, romantic side of us all, that puts us into these absurd, even ridiculous situations and positions in life. That is what the circumstances of the film are about — the theft of the necklace, the situation with the monkey, etc. All these idiotic events that one's romantic nature leads one into.*

> —Orson Welles to Henry Jaglom, in a memo from Jaglom to Jack Nicholson, dated May 20, 1982, during the efforts to launch *The Big Brass Ring*

The rift between public and private life that figures so prominently in the work of Orson Welles, from *Citizen Kane* to *The Big Brass Ring*, is ironically a factor that has tended to obscure substantial portions of his own life and work. An intensely private man himself, in spite — or should one say because? — of his expansive public image, especially during the latter portion of his life, Welles played Menaker to his own Pellarin (and vice versa) in more ways than one. While he remained in the public eye throughout his career, principally as an actor and performer, a large portion of his creative work as writer and director was kept firmly under wraps, for a number of reasons.*

If it seems likely that the closest we will ever get to a spiritual

---

*An earlier investigation into some of this work and some of these reasons can be found in my article "The Invisible Orson Welles: A First Inventory," *Sight and Sound*, Summer 1986.

autobiography of Welles will be the work he left behind, it will probably be a good many years before we can even begin to see the full shadow of his profile, much less assess it. Since his death at age 70 on October 10, 1985, it has become increasingly clear that the legacy he left behind — a wealth of material including countless films, scripts and projects, scattered over many years and countries, in different stages of completion or realization — is immeasurably larger and richer, and more full of potential surprises, than any of us had reason to suspect.

Oja Kodar — Welles's companion, muse and major collaborator over the last two decades of his life, to whom he entrusted this legacy — has dedicated herself to the formidable task of making available as much of this work as possible. But the obstacles she has to face, many of them continuations of the same financial and logistical difficulties that blocked these projects when Welles was alive, are a good deal more daunting and complex than one might initially assume. Welles essentially left behind two estates — one of them controlled by his wife Paola Mori and daughter Beatrice (complicated still further by the death of Mori in 1986), the other controlled by Kodar — and it is only recently that a final settlement has been reached. This is one reason why the publication of *The Big Brass Ring* represents a major step forward in the clarification of the invisible Orson Welles, even though it comprises only a piece of the iceberg (or jigsaw puzzle, if one prefers).

As a sample of Welles's creativity in his mid-sixties, this original screenplay offers ample evidence that he was continuing to move in fresh and unexpected directions. Yet to call it "characteristic" of his late work in any but the broadest terms would be misleading, if only because every Welles project represented a fresh departure — a virtue that regrettably kept him "unbankable" as a director throughout most of his career. Spectators looking forward to "another" *Citizen Kane* would be confounded by the challenges of *Touch of Evil*, and by the time they had caught up with the brilliance of the latter film, Welles was somewhere else again — thereby frustrating the principle of supply and demand that could sustain a Chaplin, a Hitchcock or even a Godard.

By conservative estimate, in the 1980s alone Welles was working on at least a dozen separate film projects, no two of them alike — including a film set in Hollywood in the early 1970s, *The Other Side of the Wind* (which was begun during that period), *The Magic Show* (a collection of some of his best acts of prestidigitation, all done without camera tricks), *Don Quixote* (which he had been working on intermittently since the 1950s), a fiction film about Sirhan Sirhan (*The Assassin*), adaptations of Graham Greene (*The Other Man*, based on *The Honorary Consul*) and Jim Thompson (*Dead Giveaway*, based on *A Hell of a Woman*) and Isak Dinesen (*The Dreamers*), a radically conceived *King Lear* to be shot in black and white closeups, an exercise in autobiographical self-scrutiny set in the mid-1930s (*The Cradle Will Rock*), and a development of a short story by Kodar (*Mercedes*, based on her "Blind Window") which he started work on the summer before he died. While only some of these — *The Other Side of the Wind, The Magic Show, Don Quixote* and *The Dreamers* — advanced beyond script and preproduction stages, nearly all of the scripts went through countless revisions; there are nine drafts of *The Dreamers* alone.

The Big Brass Ring was a unique project of this period insofar as it sprang from material that was completely original with Welles and was started at the urging of a friend — director Henry Jaglom — rather than at Welles's own instigation. Jaglom had already been trying without success to help Welles secure financing for *The Dreamers*, one of the latter's most cherished projects, and one day, in February or March 1981, he suggested that Welles write something more commercial and contemporary — an original script which could entice producers. After some reluctance, Welles began telling him stories over a series of lunches, and Jaglom describes the outcome as follows:

> . . . Finally he told me one he'd been thinking about for years, abo't an old political advisor to Roosevelt who was a homosexual, and wh se lover had gotten crippled in the Spanish Civil War fighting the fascists. Now he was in an African kingdom, advising the murderous leader — and back in the U.S., a young senator, who'd been his protégé, was going to run against Reagan in 1984, as the Democratic nominee. And I said, "Great! My God! That's great! Write that!" And he said, "Oh, I can't. I can't possibly." And I said, "Please write that." And he said, "No, there's no way."
>
> One night, about six days later, I got a phone call. He said, "I've got four pages." He was sweating; I could hear it: "Could I read them to you?" I said, "Sure," and he read to me — and I said, "My God, they're . . . brilliant! Please keep on writing." And he said, "What are you, crazy? It's four in the morning; I've got to go to sleep."
>
> The next day he came to lunch, and he had 12 pages. And the next day he had 23. And in three months he had a script, one which I just could not believe. It was called *The Big Brass Ring*. It was absolutely the book-end to *Citizen Kane*. It was about America at the end of the century — socially and politically and morally — as *Kane* and *Ambersons* are about America at the beginning of the century.*

After some casting about, Jaglom eventually found a willing and enthusiastic producer, Arnon Milchan, who was working at the time on *The King of Comedy* (his subsequent credits include *Once Upon a Time in America* and *Brazil*), and agreed to furnish an eight million dollar budget, pre-selling the film in foreign markets, if a "bankable" male star could be found to play Blake Pellarin. "He was amazingly clear about his job as a director in helping a producer," Milchan recalls today, remembering

---

*"The Scorpion and the Frog" by Michael Wilmington, *L.A. Style*, June 1987, Vol. 3, No. 1.

lengthy phone conversations with Welles (whom he never met face to face) on subjects ranging from technical matters about the shooting to the treatment of sex — which would be "clear and felt" but not graphic. "He was really on top of it," Milchan states with conviction.

Welles estimated that he needed six million to shoot the film — figuring on location work in Spain, filming the yacht scenes near Los Angeles, and a limited amount of studio work (possibly in Rome) for the hotel interiors — so it was decided that the remaining two million plus ten per cent of the profits would be used to lure the male star. To Milchan and Jaglom, the strategy seemed foolproof, and with Welles a list of six possible actors was drawn up: Warren Beatty, Clint Eastwood, Paul Newman, Jack Nicholson, Robert Redford and Burt Reynolds. (At earlier stages, before the "bankable" star strategy was hatched, Welles contemplated using a real-life couple to play Blake and Diana Pellarin — John Cassavetes and Gena Rowlands at one point, Cliff Robertson and Dina Merrill somewhat later; James Caan was also considered, but never approached.) But over the next year or so, they made the unhappy discovery that none of the six actors was willing to accept the offer unconditionally. Eastwood, Newman, Redford and Reynolds all simply declined, each giving a separate reason. Nicholson, who was Welles's first choice, asked for a larger sum, arguing that, after working hard for years to raise his asking price, he could not settle for two million without reducing his future fees. Beatty, Welles's second choice, fresh from having just shot *Reds*, agreed to play the part if he could produce the film and have final cut — a condition that he realized that Welles would find impossible. By late 1982, the project was effectively dead.

The version of the script printed here, the last of many drafts, is dated June 22, 1982. An undated early version, probably written about a year before, follows the same general plot outline except for one very striking difference: the climactic murder of the blind beggar is committed by Kim Menaker, not Blake Pellarin. Except for this change, the description of this scene is almost identical, apart from some echoes of the children's chant, "Quiene tiene miedo del tri-mo-tor" (sung to the tune of "Who's Afraid of the Big Bad Wolf?"), recalled earlier by Menaker in the Retiro Park — hoarsely half-whispered by Menaker as he enters the neighborhood, and later heard as a ghostly echo in his brain (along with laughter and a "scampering of little feet") after he kills the beggar.*

Although Welles ultimately chose to have Pellarin commit the murder, for a number of reasons, he significantly reassigned the crime to Menaker

---

*Kodar reports that Welles wanted to use the barely audible echo of tiny bells rather than voices to evoke this chant. Apart from this, he did not want to use many musical effects in the film; the music used would be Spanish and rather stark — basically *verbena* (fairground music) and *zarzuela* (a kind of Spanish operetta).

in one or more of the intermediate versions of the script, apparently on the basis of whether he thought the male star being approached could convincingly carry off the scene or not. The fact that he contemplated both alternatives is certainly revealing—both of the flexibility of his conception and of the larger sense that Pellarin and Menaker (like Marlow and Kurtz in *Heart of Darkness*, his first Hollywood project) are different sides of the same coin, both of them Wellesian self-portraits. It is important to recall that, like Menaker, Welles had been a friend of Franklin Roosevelt and occasionally wrote speeches for him—and that, like Pellarin, he was once regarded as a serious political hopeful, having come very close in the mid-1940s to running against Joseph McCarthy in Wisconsin as a Democrat for a seat in the Senate.

Kodar recalls a political conversation with Welles which had a particular bearing on this scene, and helps to explain one of the reasons why Pellarin (whose name, accented on the first syllable, suggests *pèlarin*, the French word for pilgrim) was the one who finally committed the crime: "You see, Orson did not like symbolism—nor do I." Once, however, he admitted to Kodar that he was guilty of symbolism in his depiction of the murder of the blind beggar. After complimenting Kodar on her smile and the whiteness of her teeth, she remarked that this was partially thanks to America, recalling the aid packages she received as a child in Yugoslavia. They then discussed the dubious wisdom of the U.S. having showered Vietnam with bombs instead of aid packages, as well as the behavior of America after destroying much of Germany and Japan in World War II, "throwing candies" at them and suffocating them with its "good intentions." At which point Welles remarked, "I'm afraid I'm going to get into some symbolism in *The Big Brass Ring*. Because this beggar is going to be killed by this enormous wealth and health."

Kodar's collaborative role on the script basically centered on the parts of Cela Brandini, which she was to play herself, and the unnamed French-Cambodian woman whom Pellarin re-encounters in an empty house. But before examining her specific contributions, it would be useful to sketch in a bit of her own background. Coming from an intellectual family grounded in the visual arts, based mainly in Dalmatia—her Hungarian father and older sister are architects, another sister paints and makes tapestries, and her Yugoslav mother wanted to be a sculptor—she aspired to be a chemist (after seeing Greer Garson in *Madame Curie*) and writer (having published poetry when she was very young) before she settled on sculpture in her teens, and was the first woman ever admitted to the sculpture department of the Academy of Visual Arts in Zagreb. Sculpting mainly in stone and bronze, and more recently in African teak, her work is at once abstract, monumental and erotic. As a reviewer in the *Tufts Observer* wrote, "Kodar conveys, through abstract forms worthy of Matisse, the human form in all its malleable transigence." She has had shows in Zagreb, Amsterdam, Paris, Rome, Boston, New York, and Los Angeles.

When she met Welles in Zagreb in 1962, while he was shooting *The Trial*, she had just finished acting in a Yugoslav feature called *A Piece of the Blue Sky*, was working as an anchorperson on Yugoslav TV, and had recently written a story called "Girl-Watching" (which years later became the Picasso episode in *F for Fake*). She accompanied Welles when he returned to Paris, but eventually left him to return to Yugoslavia. Two or three years later, she returned to Paris to attend the École des Beaux Arts, met Welles again and then remained with him for the next two decades.

Her first script collaboration with Welles was an unrealized adaptation of Poe's "The Cask of Amontillado," originally intended for a film collection of shorts by different directors, released in English as *Spirits of the Dead* in 1969. Their work together on scripts—including *F for Fake*, *The Other Side of the Wind*, *The Other Man*, *The Surinam* (an adaptation of Conrad's *Victory*), *Dead Giveaway*, *The Assassin*, *The Dreamers* and *Mercedes*—often consisted of Welles presenting a situation to her and getting her to ask questions and suggest alternatives. As she describes the process between them, it was a bit like playing pingpong; sometimes she would improvise an idea while he took notes, avoiding interruptions which would unbalance her English: "When I felt it was still too murky and too fragile to be touched or manipulated by words, I would go into my room and talk into my tape recorder. And then, when it was wrapped and safe in this little box, I would bring it out and let him listen to that, and we would talk again about it." On some occasions—including work on *F for Fake*, *The Other Side of the Wind* and *The Big Brass Ring*—it involved combining stories which each of them had composed independently.

In the case of *The Big Brass Ring*,Welles decided to incorporate certain elements from an autobiographical story written in English by Kodar seven or eight years earlier—a story which he had originally titled himself, called "Ivanka" (a Yugoslav name which means "little Joanna"). "The story of the Asian girl and part of Cela Brandini come from 'Ivanka,' " Kodar explains. "There is something of Orson and myself in the story of the Asian girl, something that we lived. It's not exactly that, but something like that happened." When Pellarin describes to Menaker over the muted noises of the feria his former lover's way of walking (page 114), this passage comes from a letter written by Welles to Kodar after they separated in Paris, a letter which was never sent, but which Welles continued to carry around with him for years, and which he showed Kodar only after he unexpectedly encountered her again in Paris. "When I met Orson again in Paris a few years later, he did not know that I was going to see him; it was a surprise. But he still had the letter, and that was the first time that I read it." One might say, in other words, that it was the Pellarin in Welles who wrote the letter, and the Menaker in him who failed to send it.

"What I had in 'Ivanka' which we decided not to use—actually he fought for it at first, and I must say I didn't want to give it to him, because

142

I was keeping it for my story—was a scene in which Blake comes up from the cellar and pours his heart out to the girl, tells her everything—and finally discovers that she's not there anymore. It's a wonderful love declaration, and in a way a love scene, but he tells it to nobody." This declaration would have been spoken in French, with English subtitles; its absence probably accounts, at least in part, for the scene's sketchiness as it now stands. "He was going to have Blake explain himself—not only what he did to her, how he hurt her and how he needed her back, but he was going to say much more about himself. He came to a certain realization of himself—what he really was—because he was in too much pain at the moment, and when people are in pain they lose control. The pain opened all the sore spots in his soul, and he was saying everything—what he thought of himself, his future and his past.

"When I took away this declaration and scene, in a way I was glad. Because I think—and actually it was Orson's decision, but he wanted my opinion—it was better for Pellarin to remain partly an enigma to himself. This is why he is capable of going off singing on that train. Because he would become a better and cleaner man, an angelic guy, if he emptied himself. But if we wanted Pellarin to continue in his striving for the Presidency, he had to remain who he was: if he confessed, if he cleaned himself, he would have been left naked, he would have lost his armor."

The character of Cela Brandini, on the other hand, was based on two independent sources. One was a somewhat comic character from "Ivanka," based on a rather flashy member of the production crew on *The Trial* who had a penchant for interviewing the directors she worked for as well as sleeping with them, and who tried unsuccessfully to seduce Welles—an event which Kodar witnessed herself. The other was the Italian journalist Oriana Fallaci, whom Kodar never met but read and watched on TV. To develop the part, she and Welles improvised scenes with a tape recorder in which her Cela would interview his Blake or Kim.

For the seasoned Welles enthusiast, *The Big Brass Ring* offers a tempting but ultimately deceptive trap: an apparent profusion of earlier touchstones in Welles's career. Starting on the first page with the evocation of *Kane* in the depiction of Pellarin's failed political campaign, the references continue with *Heart of Darkness* (page 13), Welles's radio persona (in the voice on Cela's tape recorder, preceding Welles's first appearance), *Touch of Evil* (in the opening dialogue of Jerry Kinzel on page 19 about leaving behind his wife Susie on a holiday trip) and *Don Quixote* (page 35). When Menaker remarks that, "In a perfect world, all of us should be allowed some short vacations from our own identities," the theme and world of *The Dreamers*—written just before *The Big Brass Ring*, and developed concurrently—is immediately conjured up. Even the scandalous handkerchief of Pellarin (pages 121 and 129-130) may make some readers think of the pivotal handkerchief in *Othello*.

143

Carrying this principle further, many readers will be compelled to visualize certain scenes with images gleaned from a fast-forward tour through Welles's filmography. But one should bear in mind that stylistically, Welles seldom repeated himself ("We should never borrow from ourselves," remarks Jake Hannaford, the director played by John Huston in *The Other Side of the Wind*), and at best we have to patch together our own movie out of the script rather than the one that Welles never made, which we can never hope to know. Specifically "cinematic" moments are few, although what is probably the supreme one—Menaker's voyeuristic Ferris wheel ride (pages 115-116)—might be taken as a startling metaphor for the cinema itself, bringing us all the way back to its zoetrope and peepshow origins while replicating the vicious circles of the nearby wheels of fortune and carousel; from this standpoint, the primal scene of Menaker facing the naked Pellarin, "like a great child rocking in its cradle," has the illuminating shock of a freeze-frame.

Such scenes, however, are rare, and for the most part we are obliged to read the script as a libretto for the music that Welles's direction would have brought to the material. Even more, we should acknowledge the relative poverty of our own imaginations if we should happen to think of *The Trial*, as I did, when we read, "Buildings like big ugly boxes are crammed together on the barren earth where not a tree or blade of grass is growing." When I confessed this thought to Kodar, a pragmatic anti-cinéphile with a vengeance, she responded Socratically by proposing, "Let's try to play a symbolism game. What do those buildings in *The Trial* represent to you?" After reflecting, I replied, "The crushing weight of institutions." "Yes," she said, "and what do those buildings of Franco in *The Big Brass Ring* represent to you?" Clearly, I admitted, they were not the same thing.

The moral of this story is that most of *The Big Brass Ring* comes from life, not other movies. The mention of "the illegality of the mass slaughter of the elephant" by the agreeably named Buckle (page 59) derives not from *The Roots of Heaven*, a John Huston film in which Welles acted, but from a news item which Welles and Kodar saw on television. Allusions in the dialogue to Reagan, Gay Liberation, survivalists, Kissinger, Nixon, Watergate, Vietnam and "Batunga" (identified as Uganda in an earlier draft), as well as eerie intimations of Irangate and Contragate, may create some of the newsreel immediacy of *Kane*, but their focus is the contemporary world rather than a film made in 1941. (Queried by a French film student about whether *The Big Brass Ring* would be about Reagan, Welles tersely replied, "No . . . there's not enough there for a feature movie.") A good deal more novelistic than the other Welles scripts I have read—and it is worth noting that Welles at one point planned to adapt it into a novel, exploring certain facets of the story in greater depth—it bristles with references to Welles's life, which only incidentally included the movies he made.

144

Menaker's monkey, for example, is an exact likeness, down to the same urinary disorder, of a baby wool monkey named Mimi which Welles bought in the early 1970s in a pet store on the Quai de Seine after she refused to let go of his finger, and took to the house of Kodar in Orvilliers, where the lack of proper heating made the creature miserable. Hoping that Mimi would get better in a sunnier climate, Welles took her along to Spain when he acted in (and co-wrote) *Treasure Island* — and indeed, one can see Welles with both Mimi and his pet parrot in that film — but unfortunately the cold climate in Spain made Mimi even sicker, and eventually she died of pneumonia.

It seems possible that the ambitions of Diana Pellarin for her husband were suggested in part by Paola Mori — although her "huge, tirelessly adoring eyes," resembling to Blake "a pair of lightly poached eggs," were directly inspired, according to Kodar, by Nancy Reagan. The Hasty Pudding Club Review plausibly has some relation to the early amateur theatricals of Welles at the Todd School with his teacher and lifelong friend Roger Hill. The necklace and cigarette lighter which wind up in the Mediterranean are connected to an incident involving Kodar which also found fictional form in "Ivanka," the baby eels in Menaker's beard can be traced back to a meal with Henri Langlois in Barcelona, and even the "prestigious firm of Pellarin, Loeb, Leibowitz and Cirello" [*sic*] (page 70) has some autobiographical significance in its nod to Welles's loyal chauffeur in the 1940s, a hunchbacked dwarf named "Shorty" Chirello.

Similarly, the deserted house with covered furniture where Blake meets his long-lost lover, along with the carnival and fireworks outside,* were suggested by specific places where Welles and Kodar had stayed in Spain and France. More generally, the importance of the Spanish Civil War in the script can be related to Welles's own intense political involvements during that period, which led to him being labelled (along with certain other leftists) a "premature antifascist"; Kodar points out that he surely would have fought in that war if his poor health had not excluded the possibility.

By contrasting the Spanish Civil War with Vietnam, Welles is doing something more than juxtaposing the moral watersheds of two generations some thirty years apart. The lost lovers of Menaker and Pellarin alike are viewed as casualties of those wars, and the libidinal sense of guilt and irrationality which charges through the screenplay like a live wire — culminating in Pellarin's murder of the blind beggar — underlines the relations between the powerful and the powerless, the haves and the have nots, which inform the plot like variations on a musical theme. From Tina

---

*Developing a bold idea first sketched out in the prologue to *Heart of Darkness*, Welles planned to show the reflected lights of the fireworks in the room where Blake rejoins his lover *in color* — a unique moment in an otherwise black and white film. References to the "little color bombs" and "colored lights" on page 118 suggest that color may have been used there as well.

(the Portuguese maid) to the monkey to the boy asleep in the Retiro Park to Vanni to the French-Cambodian woman to the blind beggar, the gallery of the helpless confronting Menaker and Pellarin register like phantoms of liberal guilt as well as agents of their tortured trajectories. For all the big shots surrounding the two leads, most of them comic grotesques, it is these marginal figures who form the major pivots of the narrative, propelling the heroes forward.

While Cela Brandini might initially seem to belong to the haves rather than the have nots, she is in fact the only go-between, serving as the reader/spectator's guide into the world of the film. Significantly, she is the only European character in the film who speaks at any length. While she shares with Menaker and Pellarin an international status, she remains a perpetual outsider, serving as the film's European conscience (and consciousness). Like the others, she is left behind at the station while the American innocents charge off, scot-free—despite the blood and semen on their hands—to their elusive destinies.

Playing against the contemporaneous aspects of *The Big Brass Ring* are many facets of Welles's artistic personality which seem to belong to earlier historical periods. In one of the most suggestive recent essays about Welles, "The Force of the Work" by Bill Krohn—available in French as the Introduction to *Cahiers du Cinéma*'s most recent special Welles issue "*hors-serie*," but unfortunately unpublished in English—it is argued that his art expresses a nostalgia for the Middle Ages on many different levels: the "economy governing [his] system of production . . . resembles the economy of feudalism," his form of storytelling evolves from that of the resident farmer to that of the trading seaman (forms which "intermingled for the first time in the medieval trading cities"), and "the popular 'carnivalesque' forms of the Middle Ages" are reflected throughout his films—not only in such obvious instances as *Don Quixote* and *Chimes at Midnight*, but elsewhere as well. Formally his films "recreate the *scene* of the carnival, where disparate members of society collide, commingle and converse"; thematically they recreate what Mikhail Bakhtin calls "the great carnival theme, 'the pathos of shifts and changes' evoked by the crowning and uncrowning of a mock king . . ."—a process that brings to mind Menaker as well as Pellarin.

At the same time, it should be noted that *The Big Brass Ring* seems equally grounded in Anglo-American fiction of the nineteenth century. Even without the mediating narration of a Marlow, the guilt-ridden darkness of Pellarin and Menaker suggests the universe of Conrad, and it is worth recalling that Welles's script adaptations of *Heart of Darkness*, *Lord Jim* and *Victory* span three decades of his career. On another plane, the gallery of fools comprising Pellarin's political entourage owes something to the caricatural energy of Dickens—think of the aforementioned J. Sheldon Buckle, or Dinty Benart—reminding one that a *Pickwick Papers* with W.C. Fields was one of Welles's earliest Hollywood projects.

Against these European antecedents, one must also consider the spirit of Mark Twain, especially *Tom Sawyer* and *Huckleberry Finn* (the latter of which was adapted into one of the most brilliant of Welles's radio shows). Clearly the childish mischief of Pellarin and Menaker belongs to a myth of freedom and innocent intrigue that relates to Huck and Jim's raft and the male camaraderie it fosters, while some of the more gratuitous and contrived capers of Pellarin evoke certain machinations of Tom. The bittersweet ending of the departure on the train ("If you want a happy ending, that depends, of course, on where you stop your story") carries some of the ambiguity inherent in Huck's closing words, and the very title of the screenplay conjures up a child's playful endeavor and hellbent toy vehicle which belong in the company of Charlie Kane's sled and Georgie Minafer's carriage.

Yet in spite of all this literary parentage, it could be argued that the acuteness of Welles's grasp of international politics and blustering American dominance reveals a maturity of moral viewpoint that is less apparent in the flippant references to Kane's war-mongering and other forms of demagoguery over four decades earlier. Without the benefit of charismatic performances and concrete images, the screenplay belongs to literature more than film history, and on that level it certainly bears comparison with the depiction of power and solitude essayed by Welles and Herman J. Mankiewicz. The enigma of personality is no less apparent, and a sense of America existing in the world rather than within the confines of its own solipsism suggests a broader and more sophisticated frame of reference.

"I'm bored with stories that don't seem to be balanced dangerously," Welles remarked in a 1981 interview, speaking about *The Lady from Shanghai.* "If you walk down a highway with a story instead of on a tightrope, I'm bored with it." The sense of reckless danger informing both the writing of *The Big Brass Ring* and the action contained inside it testifies to the fierce persistence of Welles's creativity and nerve, in defiance of the industry's conservatism and cowardice that kept him unemployed as a Hollywood director over the last twenty-eight years of his life, at the same time that he was almost universally revered as his country's greatest filmmaker.

The desire to shock is as palpable here as in the seediness and violence of *Touch of Evil*, which even in 1958 was the first Hollywood film he had been able to make since *Macbeth*, an experimental three-week cheapie shot at Republic studios a decade earlier. (In the interim, Welles had embarked on the alternative route of financing his own filmmaking with *Othello* — a dangerous departure in its own right, but one that proved to yield more results than his efforts to work within the Hollywood system.)

Clearly not all of Welles's late works carry this rebellious and daring spirit — although reportedly portions of the still unfinished *The Other Side the Wind*, which Kodar and cinematographer Gary Graver are determined to complete, are equally hair-raising and unexpected. Judging only by the screenplays that I have read, *The Cradle Will Rock*, apart from its elements of autocritique, is surprisingly benign towards its characters, while *The Dreamers* reads like the apotheosis of Welles's lyricism and romanticism. According to both Kodar and Jaglom, Welles felt personally closer to *The Dreamers* than to *The Big Brass Ring*, which leads one to the intriguing yet paradoxical postulate that he tended to identify more with his adaptations than with his original scripts — *The Magnificent Ambersons* rather than *Citizen Kane*, *Chimes at Midnight* rather than *Mr. Arkadin*. Perhaps this can be attributed to the Sancho Panza side of his personality — the desire to locate himself within an existing world rather than construct an alternative one. But as the Wellesian oeuvre continues to expand, even after his death, in all directions, with a frenzy of invention that will keep us chasing after its meanings for years to come, altering our sense of the works we already know, *The Big Brass Ring* allows us the rare privilege of hearing his voice, resonant and unmistakable, still in the present, addressing us directly.

JONATHAN ROSENBAUM